TRUTH or TRADITION

Rediscovering the Truth About God, About Us, and How Salvation <u>Really</u> Works

By
Les Leno

TEACH Services, Inc.
P U B L I S H I N G
www.TEACHServices.com • (800) 367-1844

World rights reserved. This book or any portion thereof may not be copied or reproduced in any form or manner whatever, except as provided by law, without the written permission of the publisher, except by a reviewer who may quote brief passages in a review.

The author assumes full responsibility for the accuracy of all facts and quotations as cited in this book. The opinions expressed in this book are the author's personal views and interpretations, and do not necessarily reflect those of the publisher.

This book is provided with the understanding that the publisher is not engaged in giving spiritual, legal, medical, or other professional advice. If authoritative advice is needed, the reader should seek the counsel of a competent professional.

Copyright © 2014 Les Leno
Copyright © 2014 TEACH Services, Inc.
ISBN-13: 978-1-47960-239-1 (Paperback)
ISBN-13: 978-1-47960-240-7 (ePub)
ISBN-13: 978-1-47960-241-4 (Mobi)
Library of Congress Control Number: 2013949126

Published by

www.TEACHServices.com • (800) 367-1844

All scripture quotations, unless otherwise indicated, are taken from the New King James Version®. Copyright © 1982 by Thomas Nelson, Inc. Used by permission. All rights reserved.

Scripture quotations marked GNB are from the Good News Bible, The Bible in Today's English Version, Second Edition Copyright © 1992 by American Bible Society. Used by Permission.

Scripture quotations marked Goodspeed are taken from The New Testament by Edgar J. Goodspeed. Copyright © 1923 by The University of Chicago.

Scripture quotations marked ISV are taken from The Holy Bible: International Standard Version®. Copyright © 1996-forever by The ISV Foundation. ALL RIGHTS RESERVED INTERNATIONALLY. Used by permission.

Scripture quotations marked KJV are taken from the King James Version. Public domain.

Scripture quotations marked LB are taken from The Living Bible, copyright © 1971 by Tyndale House Publishers, Wheaton, Ill. 60187. Used by permission.

Scripture quotations marked MSG are from THE MESSAGE. Copyright © by Eugene H. Peterson 1993, 1994, 1995, 1996, 2000, 2001, 2002. Used by permission of NavPress Publishing Group.

Scripture quotations marked NASB are taken from the New American Standard Bible®, Copyright © 1960, 1962, 1968, 1971, 1972, 1973, 1975, 1977, 1995 by The Lockman Foundation. Used by permission.

Scripture quotations marked NEB are taken from The New English Bible. Copyright © 1961, 1970. Used by permission of Oxford University Press and Cambridge University Press. All rights reserved worldwide.

Scripture quotations marked NIV are taken from the Holy Bible, New International Version®, NIV®. Copyright © 1973, 1978, 1984, 2011 by Biblica, Inc.™ Used by permission of Zondervan. All rights reserved worldwide.

Scripture quotations marked NIrV are taken from the Holy Bible, NEW INTERNATIONAL READER'S VERSION®. Copyright © 1996, 1998 Biblica. All rights reserved throughout the world. Used by permission of Biblica.

Scripture quotations marked NLT are taken from The Holy Bible, New Living Translation copyright © 1996. Used by permission of Tyndale House Publishers, Wheaton, Ill. 60189. All rights reserved.

Scripture quotations marked NRSV are taken from New Revised Standard Version Bible, copyright 1989, Division of Christian Education of the National Council of the Churches of Christ in the United States of America. Used by permission. All rights reserved.

Scripture quotations marked NTMS are taken from the New Testament in Modern Speech, 5th Edition by Richard Francis Weymouth. Copyright © 1929, published by James Clarke & Co., LTD, London.

Scripture quotations marked Phillips are taken from J. B. Phillips, "The New Testament in Modern English," 1962 edition, published by HarperCollins.

Scripture quotations marked Rieu are taken from The Four Gospels translated by E.V. Rieu. Copyright © 1953 by Penguin Press.

Scripture quotations marked RV are taken from the Revised Version. Public domain.

Scripture quotations marked TCNT are taken from The Twentieth Century New Testament, revised edition. Copyright © 1904 by Fleming H. Revell Co.

Scripture quotations marked WNT are taken from the Weymouth New Testament. Public domain.

Contents

About This Book vii
1. The Law 9
2. Sin 14
3. Sinful Nature 16
4. Repentance 19
5. Acceptance 23
6. Forgiveness 26
7. Obedience 31
8. Perfection 36
9. Grace 39
10. Faith 42
11. Salvation 47
12. Justification 51
13. Righteousness 55
14. Justice 57
15. Works 61
16. Intercession 65
17. Legalism 70
18. Atonement 74
19. Sanctification 84
20. The Gospel 87
21. Allegiance 93
22. Putting It All Together 96
Appendix: Why God Commanded Love 99

About This Book

We're no different than the people of Christopher Columbus' day. Of course we don't believe the world is flat, but we, too, hold deeply engrained beliefs that aren't true. Especially the beliefs we hold about God. To make matters worse, because of the prevalent views of our culture and what we have been taught, any thought as to the truth of what we believe bypasses our conscious thinking, and we go on thinking what we've always thought. As a result, we pass on these false beliefs to our children. Thus, they become more and more engrained with each successive generation.

It's no wonder, then, that in a nationwide survey of adults' spiritual beliefs, The Barna Group found that Americans who consider themselves Christian have a varied set of beliefs, many of which are contradictory or, at least, inconsistent.

This should be of great concern, for from these beliefs we get our opinions about God. They determine how we relate to Him, profoundly influence how we think He relates to us, and define how we think salvation works.

The purpose of this book is to examine some of the major teachings of the Christian faith and reach for the real truth that lies hidden beneath layers of tradition and misinterpretation. One might think that the teaching in the first chapter, "The Law," is well understood. And it should be, because it is absolutely foundational to the Christian belief system. But this may be the most misunderstood teaching of all.

Chapter 1
THE LAW

From the day we met, Merle and I shared a passion for things with wheels. It began with toy cars in the dirt, and then turned to bicycles as soon as we were able to ride. We not only experimented with all kinds of strange configurations, but the way we rode these contraptions also deviated from the norm. With reckless speed and daring stunts we "terrorized" the citizens of our small town. We never hurt anybody, but I suspect we scared a few people half to death.

Then it was wheels with engines. Though not old enough to have drivers' licenses, we began our first major project—to build a hot rod. We bought an old '32 Ford, and after removing the body from the frame, we were well on our way to our dream. We toiled long and hard with eager anticipation of the day it would be completed. But long before it was done our enthusiasm got the better of us. We just had to test drive it. Strapping a makeshift seat to the bare frame, we were off. The roar and raw power of the unmuffled V-8 along with the sound of tires screaming for traction was a real adrenaline rush. Wow! Was this great or what? Our fun didn't last long though. Someone reported us to the police and we were soon arrested. The crime: driving a "car" with no license, no muffler, no lights, no fenders, no windshield, and no body. We were doomed. In due course the judgment was set and the books were opened.

With crippling fear and anxiety we awaited our sentencing in the awful silence of the cold courtroom. Our mothers beside us, suffered in quiet shame and humiliation. We had no one to plead our case, and we were found guilty as charged. Oh how we prayed for grace from the stern-faced judge on high. I'd like to say he pardoned us, but he showed no mercy. Punishment was imposed, and we paid the penalty for our crimes.

Humanity's Laws Versus God's Law

Real life experiences like this (except with better outcomes) are often used to illustrate how God's law and grace operate in our lives. The worse the crime, the better the illustration. The best ones are condemned-to-die criminals who were pardoned and set free. We've all heard them, and they sound so right. But these illustrations give the impression that the nature of God's law is no different than man's laws. They suggest that the Ten Commandments are like speed limits and tax laws—arbitrarily imposed rules that carry no consequence for violation unless penalties are also imposed. Thus the character of the Lawgiver is maligned. And because the law is so fundamental to the Christian belief system, misunderstanding its nature causes our understanding of most, if not all, other tenets of our faith to become flawed. It's like the Leaning Tower of Pisa. Because the foundation is faulty, all the rooms are out of kilter. Let me explain.

Two Types of Laws

Understanding the difference between people's laws and God's law requires some technical explanation. Now, I don't want you to get bogged down here and quit, so bear with me for just a bit. Two types of laws affect us all. One is "imposed" or "prescribed," and the other is "fixed," "natural," or "descriptive." Imposed laws are man-made. These laws are simply made-up rules that can be changed or done away with at any time. They are forced on us and deal strictly with *external behavior and punishment*: "Do this, and don't do that—or else." The penalties threatened are designed to produce sufficient fear to motivate us to obey. If we do not obey, we will be appropriately punished—that is, if we get caught.

In a hurry to get home one night we passed a police car hiding by the side of the road. I didn't see it, but my wife did and immediately said something like, "You're in trouble now."

"Why?" I asked.

"Because you just passed a cop back there and you were going over the speed limit," she replied. But as we anxiously watched in our rearview mirrors we were relieved to find that we were not being pursued. Either the cop didn't notice my speed or chose not to come after me. As a result I suffered no consequence for breaking the law. I'll refer to laws in this category as "rules."

Descriptive Law

The second type of law is what scientists call "descriptive" or "natural" law. These laws exist as a natural part of our universe and are binding on everything everywhere. From atoms to galaxies, everything animate and inanimate is governed by some kind of descriptive law. Some of these laws are "distant" from us and we do not encounter them directly. But many, like the law of gravity, are so much a part of our everyday lives that we hardly notice they are there. These laws are as fixed and unchangeable as time itself. Unlike imposed rules that can be set aside or even ignored without consequence when no one is looking, descriptive laws are *the invariable way things behave*, or, *what inevitably occurs under given conditions*. I'll refer to the laws in this category as "natural, descriptive or fixed law."

Moral Law

While most people recognize the existence and operation of natural law in the physical realm, few seem to be aware that a descriptive law exists in the moral realm as well. The moral realm is the realm of our minds, and the law is this: what we experience affects us psychologically and physiologically. In other words, what we see, hear, feel and even say, actually reacts on our minds.

This is not just my idea. In the November 11, 1996, issue of *U.S. News and World Report*, several scientific studies were cited that suggest that this is indeed true. Researchers discovered that unloving behavior, like neglect and abuse, actually altered the architecture of children's brains and how they functioned. This resulted in a variety of disturbances in physiology, thinking, and behavior. The minds of adults are similarly affected. When we don't love, and/or are not loved, it affects our minds and the minds of others. I'll refer to this law as "moral law."

What Does All This Have to Do with the Ten Commandments?

Everything. When Christ reduced the Ten Commandments to two, He made it clear that they are all about love. "'Love the Lord your God with all your heart and with all your soul and with all your mind,'" He said. "This is the first and greatest commandment. And the second is like it: 'Love your neighbor as yourself.' *All the Law and the Prophets hang on these two commandments*" (Matt. 22:37–40, NIV, emphasis mine).

Now, because these are *commandments,* many get the idea that they are imposed rules. But making a rule cannot create love. Instead of being imposed rules that call for penalties to be imposed on the violator, the Ten Commandment law is inextricably linked to the descriptive moral law in a cause-effect relationship. Here's how it works: suppose God gave us a rule on how to relate to the law of gravity. What if He commanded, "Thou shalt not jump out of tall buildings?" Would that command make the law of gravity an imposed law? No. Why not? Because, the "penalty" for disregarding this theoretical command is not imposed. It is a *natural consequence* inherent in the law of gravity.

On September 11, 2001, I sat glued to the images on the TV in my hotel room as I watched in horror and disbelief at the terror and devastation at the World Trade Center. With gut-wrenching emotion I watched the sickening scene of petrified people who apparently chose to jump from the Towers and smash into the ground rather than die in the inferno above. Did God impose punishment on those poor people for the way they related to one of His descriptive laws? Of course not, it was a natural consequence of their actions.

The relationship between the hypothetical command not to jump off tall buildings and the law of gravity is the same that exists between the Ten Commandment law and the moral law. God gave us the commandments because there are serious consequences for relating to the moral law in the wrong way. We needed them because when we relate to God and each other in wrong ways, bad things inevitably happen—to us and to others.

What Difference Does It Make How I View the Law?

Nothing effects our relationship with God more than a how we view the law. This is absolutely pivotal because it subtly influences our opinion of the Lawgiver, how we *think* He relates to us, and in turn, determines how we relate to Him. If I see the law as rules, it follows that I will believe that God must and will impose a penalty for breaking the rules. This paints Him as arbitrary, capricious, and exacting, and either leads to all manner of legalism, or to a total rejection of a vengeful God who threatens to torture you in hell if you don't accept what He has to offer or do what He says.

On the other hand, if I understand the true nature of the law, I see that God is trying to protect His children from harm, and I relate to Him altogether differently. I realize He is looking out for my best good and is *infinitely* loving and compassionate. I also realize that with Him who said "love your enemies" (Luke 6:27) "there is never the slightest variation or shadow of inconsistency" (James 1:17, Phillips). Comprehending the true nature of the law causes me to see sin in a different light too. And this is the subject of our next chapter.

(For a discussion on why God commanded us to love when He knows that it cannot be produced by command, and why He gave the commandments in such a fearsome way, please see the appendix.)

Chapter 2
SIN

When babies begin talking they often come up with funny names for things. Our daughter was no exception. She had her own words for "airplane" and "banana" and they had no recognizable similarity to anything in the English language—or any other language for that matter. But we knew to what she was referring. The word "sin" is like that. It's just a word, a noun that stands for something, a term that we use to help us know to what we're referring. Though Christians and non-Christians both use this term, not all agree as to what sin actually is. Many believe sin is "breaking the rules," and that seems consistent with 1 John 3:4, which defines sin as "transgression of the law." But since the law is not imposed, what does it mean to transgress it?

Paul says, "love is the fulfilling of the law" (Rom. 13:10, KJV). So if love fulfills the requirements of the law, wouldn't transgression of the law be the opposite of loving, and therefore sin? And this is exactly what is implied in 1 Corinthians 13: "I may be able to speak the languages of human beings and even of angels, but if I have no love, my speech is no more than a noisy gong or a clanging bell." (*I am still a transgressor of the law.*) "I may have the gift of inspired preaching; I may have all knowledge and understand all secrets; I may have all the faith needed to move mountains—but if I have no love, I am nothing." (*I would still be a transgressor of the law.*) "I may give away everything I have, and even give up my body to be burned—but if I have no love, this does me no good" (1 Cor. 13:1-3, GNB). (*I still remain a transgressor of the law.*)

The parable of the Good Samaritan is also consistent with this definition of sin. Though Christ primarily told this story to answer the question, "Who is our neighbor?" it also shows that the priest and the Levite sinned because they did nothing to help the unfortunate man at the side of the road. Apparently this lesson was not lost on James because he later said, "to him that knoweth to do good, and doeth it not, to him it is sin" (James 4:17, KJV).

Sin Is Not Just Behavior

So in a technical sense, sin *is* "transgression of the law." But this does not mean it is limited to behavior only—what you see on the outside. Sin can be visible on the outside or hidden on the inside. It can be doing things or not doing things, or just an attitude. It can be apathy, indifference, or outright rebellion. Sin is anything that is not consistent with love and since God is love it separates us from Him. *Sin is any thought, desire, inclination, attitude, motive, emotion, word, or action that is not of a loving nature. It is the outworking of a principle that is at war with the law of love.*

"Emotions can be sin?" you ask.

Yes.

"But," you say, "we have no control over our emotions."

Exactly right. Though we can try to stifle them, and keep them from showing on the outside, we can't control what's happening on the inside. They are too much a part of who we are. Furthermore, although we are commanded to love, we can't *make* ourselves love our enemies even if we want to. Why is this? And what can be done about it? The answer to the first question comes in understanding our next subject—fallen, sinful, human nature. Don't despair. There *is* a solution.

Chapter 3
SINFUL NATURE

Once upon a time a scorpion and a frog chanced upon each other on the banks of a wide, flowing river. After some wary chitchat they discovered their mutual desire to get to the other side. The scorpion, being unable to swim, tried to persuade the frog to ferry him across. But the frog was afraid that the scorpion would sting him in the process, so he was adamantly against the idea. After discussing the matter at some length, the scorpion finally said, "Look, I won't sting you. I'd be stupid to do such a thing. If I did, of course you'd die, but I would too. I'd drown because I can't swim."

The argument made sense to the frog, so he agreed. The scorpion climbed onto the frog's back and off they went. Halfway across the river the scorpion gave the frog a fatal sting. As the frog, writhing in agony, began to sink, he cried out, "Why did you sting me? You promised not to." And the scorpion, as he too was going to his grave, replied, "I couldn't help it. It's my nature."

What About Us?

Considering our bent to embrace evil, and how we've just defined sin, it is evident that our problem is bigger than merely committing sinful acts. The apostle Paul understood this when he said, "I know I am rotten through and through so far as my old sinful nature is concerned. No matter which way I turn I can't make myself do right" (Rom. 7:18, NLT). He knew that "the mind governed by the flesh is hostile to God; it does not submit to God's law, nor can it do so" (Rom. 8:7, NIV). David also recognized this when he said, "From the time I was conceived, I have been sinful" (Ps. 51:5, GNB).

When we were born, our natural tendencies and inclinations were not toward loving thoughts and selfless behavior. As innocent as we may have looked, it wasn't long before the real truth was evident. No one had to teach us how to be selfish, or how to respond in kind when another child hit us. And as we got older, it didn't get any better.

In their day, the Pharisees tried to cure the problem by making more rules. But Christ said, "You have heard that it was said to the people long ago, 'You shall not murder, and anyone who murders will be subject to judgment.' But I tell you that anyone who is angry with a brother or sister will be subject to judgment.... You have heard that it was said, 'You shall not commit adultery.' But I tell you that anyone who looks at a woman lustfully has already committed adultery with her in his heart" (*mind*) (Matt. 5:21–28, NIV).

In essence Christ was saying to the Jews, "You've got it all wrong. The sin problem isn't about external acts; it has to do with your mind. That's where the problem is." His own disciples didn't get it either, so Jesus pressed this truth home with a more pointed statement. "Don't you understand?" He asked. "From the *heart* come evil thoughts, murder, adultery, fornication, theft, lying and slander" (Matt. 15:16, 19, NLT, emphasis mine). Of course He was not referring to our blood pumpers, but to our minds.

Our Minds Are Like Computers

When God created Adam and Eve, their minds were similar to computer hard drives with good, clean programs already installed. They functioned and interfaced with each other perfectly. But since they had the power of choice, they had complete control over what they did with their "hard drives." Sadly, Eve believed the slick marketing message of an evil competitor who convinced her she needed a bigger "database." Adam too decided to buy the "program," and they each "downloaded" what they considered to be an "upgrade." But the "upgrade program" manufactured by this con man had a "virus" in it, and by the time they realized it, it was too late. The damage was done. When they made "copies" of themselves, the "virus" passed from one "hard drive" to another. Consequently, we all have a contaminated "hard drive." Left alone, eventually our whole system will crash. Meanwhile, because of garbage in, it's garbage out.

It's in Our Genes

The reality is we were born with desires and inclinations that cause us to think and act in unloving ways. Ways that are ultimately destructive. It's our nature—our sinful nature. We're "sick" in the head. And if we do not acknowledge this, and seek help from the Doctor, the prognosis is terminal. "For if we take up the attitude 'we have not sinned,' we flatly deny God's diagnosis of *our condition* and cut ourselves off from what he has to say to us" (1 John 1:10, Phillips, emphasis mine).

So our "sinful nature" is a condition of the mind that produces thoughts, desires, attitudes, emotions, motives, words and actions that are out of harmony with the principle of love. It's a mental "disease." But there is hope, for there is a Great Physician.

Chapter 4
REPENTANCE

After Merle and I received our punishment that dark day in court (oddly, I don't remember what it was), we were definitely repentant. Not because we were sorry for doing something wrong, but because we got caught and punished. After all, we were good drivers. We'd been careful, and we hadn't hurt anyone, and it was all innocent fun, and, and, and ... And every subsequent time I earned a traffic citation I was sorry again—for being caught. The truth is, I possessed and nurtured a rebellious attitude. I still wanted to drive the way I wanted to drive, and I felt justified in continuing my behavior. I would just have to be more careful. Obviously my repentance was not genuine.

What Is Genuine Repentance?

Now suppose that after being caught, the punishment made me sorry enough to change my behavior. And though I didn't really want to, I would obey the law. Would that be true repentance? Let's consider the apparent repentance of Judas and Peter. Both betrayed Christ. After Judas' betrayal, he said, "I have sinned ... for I have betrayed innocent blood" (Matt. 27:4, NIV). Was his repentance genuine? No. His admission came when he realized that Christ was not going to exert His power to free Himself, set Himself up as the new king, and stomp the Romans. I believe this confession was forced from him by an awful sense of condemnation in a coming judgment.

But Peter's repentance was different. His was not from fear of punishment, but from a heart full of genuine sorrow. When he denied Christ the third time and the rooster crowed, Christ looked at Peter with such love, forgiveness, and pity that it broke his heart. Peter suddenly saw himself as he really was and he abhorred himself for doing what he did to his Best Friend. Peter's repentance was genuine, and he went on to become a mighty witness to the forgiving love of Christ.

Judas had the same opportunity when Jesus washed his dirty feet. Though Jesus knew what he was up to, He showed Judas the same love and forgiveness He showed Peter. But Judas showed "contempt for the riches of his kindness, tolerance and patience" (Rom. 2:4, NIV). Instead of truly repenting, he went ahead with his diabolical plan, then went out and hanged himself.

A Personal Experience of Repentance

I'm ashamed to admit it even took place, but this personal incident illustrates what I believe to be genuine repentance. It happened some years ago while driving in busy downtown Seattle. Proceeding on a green light, I could not clear the intersection because of a pedestrian in the crosswalk. While he leisurely sauntered his way across the street I waited patiently—for a moment or two. Then my light turned red and a whole street full of traffic descended upon me with horns blaring. Waiting for the pedestrian, I was blocking everyone else.

At that point this man realized he had complete control of the whole intersection. Visibly enjoying the power of it all, he modified his gait to a slow swagger. When he was directly in front of my car, I lost it. With the transmission already in first gear, I shoved the gas pedal to the floor and popped the clutch. Not just momentarily. I meant business, and I didn't let up. How he ever managed to jump far and fast enough to escape being run over I'll never know.

Seething inside, I continued down the street. Then, in my thoughts, the Holy Spirit began to work on me. *You could have killed that man.*

My response was one of self-justification. *But you saw what he did. He had it coming.*

But the Holy Spirit persisted. *You did it on purpose. You're a murderer at heart.*

But he deliberately did it to cause me a problem, I responded.

The Holy Spirit responded back, *If he hadn't been so agile you would have killed him. You're a murderer.*

But he had no right to do what he did.

You're a murderer, the Holy Spirit said again.

But ... I said.

You're a murderer, the Holy Spirit stated.

But ... I weakly said.

You're a murderer came the thought again.

But ... I tried one last time.

You're a murderer was the response.

Thankfully, the Holy Spirit persisted until in brokenness of spirit I acknowledged the truth of what He was saying. I saw the sinfulness of my heart and admitted that I was capable of murder. I was appalled at my attitude and behavior and realized my need of Christ. I wanted to be changed on the inside so that my desires, motives, feelings, and emotions would be in harmony with the commandment to love. True repentance had come.

We Need to Repent of More Than Wrong Acts

Repentance is more easily understood when applied to individual acts of wrongdoing. And so far we have only been looking at it in this context. But repentance means more than merely regretting our wrongful acts. We need to repent of our condition.

"Our condition?" you ask. "Wait a minute, why should I repent of my condition? I never asked to be born, much less in this condition. I didn't have a choice."

True, but to repent of your condition doesn't imply you caused it. It just means you've come face to face with it and acknowledge who you are—a created being, "infected" and "sick," with an unloving nature.

In either case, be it repentance for our condition or for wrongful acts, we cannot conjure up genuine repentance on our own. It comes from above. The apostle Paul says it is the goodness of God that draws us to repentance (Rom. 2:4, WNT). But *we* determine whether or not it becomes a reality within us. And this is where the rubber meets the road. When the Holy Spirit convicts us of our wrongful acts or sick condition, and brings to our consciousness our helplessness and deep need, we can either deny the truth, try to justify ourselves in our own eyes and thereby cut ourselves off from what He has to say to us, or we can say yes to the Spirit, admit the truth of what He is saying and reach out to God for healing. If the latter is the case, we have experienced genuine repentance.

True Repentance

True repentance includes a genuine remorse for our individual acts of wrongdoing, an acknowledgement of our condition, and the turning from sin and coming to God for healing. But to turn away from sin does not imply we can change our nature. It means a change in our thinking, making the decision and choosing to have nothing to do with sin in any form—visible or invisible, intentional or unintentional. And, praise God, "The Lord is not slack concerning his promise, as some men count slackness; but is longsuffering to us-ward, not willing that any should perish, but that all should come to repentance" (2 Peter 3:9, KJV).

Chapter 5
ACCEPTANCE

Though there is general agreement that God accepts everyone just the way they are, I've found there are differing opinions as to what God's acceptance actually means. In everyday life we use this term in a variety of ways. We accept something given to us; we accept the way things are; we accept compliments; and we accept someone's love. In these contexts the meaning of the word "acceptance" is clear. But acceptance, when applied to our relationship with God, apparently is a different matter.

In relationships, acceptance or non-acceptance is something *shown* or *communicated* in some way. We can see it in the interaction of others or experience it personally when we come into someone's presence or interact with them in one way or another. There's a familiar old story that illustrates true acceptance.

A man enters through the main doors of a church and slowly makes his way down the center aisle, searching for an empty seat. His dress and appearance are drastically different from the pious members sitting in the pews. His hair is long, dirty, and unkempt. His clothes are ragged and soiled. As he goes, every head turns to look at this pathetic specimen of humanity who dares to intrude their sanctuary. Not finding an empty seat anywhere, or anyone who will make room for him, he eventually finds himself at the front of the church where he sits down on the floor directly in front of the pulpit. A murmuring stir ripples through the congregation as the members reveal their thoughts.

Promptly another man makes his way down the aisle. Again, all heads turn. This time it's the deacon in charge. He will deal with the situation. Breathlessly, all watch as he reaches his target. Laying a hand on the intruder's shoulder, the deacon sinks to the floor, sits down cross-legged beside him, and extends a warm welcome. Who showed acceptance? Who demonstrated non-acceptance?

Acceptance Is Having an Affirming Attitude Toward Others

The opposite of acceptance is rejection or disapproval. Have you ever known someone in whose presence you felt judged, condemned, or censured? Have you felt their frown upon you, felt that they viewed you with disfavor, found fault with you, or criticized you? That's non-acceptance. Acceptance is seeing others as having value and affirming them. It's communicating a loving attitude toward them despite what they do or don't do, how they look, what they wear or don't wear, what they think or don't think. Someone once told me he felt it necessary to withhold love from his son and daughter when he did not approve of their behavior.

"Otherwise," he said, "I would be seen as condoning it." Consequently, they felt condemned, unloved, and rejected. Which of the above descriptions fits how God views us? Does God withhold love because of our behavior, or because of our condition?

God's Acceptance

Christ's story of the prodigal son is a powerful illustration of how God the Father feels about us. Regardless of our behavior, when we come to Him there is no censure, no reprimands, and no reminders of what we are or what we've done. God the Father simply offers unconditional, loving acceptance of us. Christ (who said, "He who has seen Me has seen the Father" [John 14:9]) also demonstrated some incredible acts of acceptance, mirroring the Father's love for His children. Look how He treated Judas. Although He knew that Judas was an unsalvageable traitor, it didn't change His love and attitude of acceptance toward Judas in the slightest. And look how Jesus treated Peter after the way Peter treated Him. And Mary. And the demoniacs. And all the sick and diseased people. He loved, accepted, and healed everyone who came, in spite of the fact that many had only themselves to blame for their condition. Because He did, the sanctimonious Jews said, "This man eats with sinners." And they had no idea of the beautiful truth of their statement.

Does Acceptance by God Mean We're Saved?

Because God accepts us unconditionally when we come to Him, many equate acceptance with salvation. But from the experience of Judas, and the rich young ruler, we see this can't be true. Yes, He is always loving and accepting, but h*ow we respond* to Him determines whether or not we're saved.

In essence, *God's acceptance is His attitude of love and approval toward us, the opposite of condemnation, repulsion, and rejection.* And regardless of our behavior or our condition, He still loves and accepts everyone who comes to Him. We are His children and He will never reject or withhold love from His children—*any* of His children— no matter what! He says, "whoever comes to me I will never drive away" (John 6:37, NIV). "Accept one another, then, just as Christ has accepted you" (Rom. 15:7, NIV).

Chapter 6
FORGIVENESS

Because the word "forgiveness" is so common in everyday language, and its meaning well understood, it may seem like a waste of time to discuss it. But if we bring this common everyday meaning into the realm of religion we may be embracing something the devil himself would be happy for us to believe. Let me explain.

Webster's New Collegiate Dictionary says that to forgive means "to cease to feel resentment (against an offender)." In other words, to no longer hold anything against someone. Since our usage of the term seems consistent with this definition, what's the problem? There isn't when this meaning is applied to human relationships. But this is not an accurate reflection of what goes on between God and us.

If God's law were simply imposed rules, Webster's definition would fit precisely. But considering the true nature of the law and our "sick" condition, this brand of forgiveness doesn't make sense when applied to our relationship with God. For instance, let's suppose a man is unfaithful to his wife, and as a result, he gets AIDS. After he is infected, he infects his wife. Subsequently they have children, and tests show they are all born HIV positive. Do the children need forgiveness? Will forgiveness make them well? Should we hold resentment against them for what their father did? Should we punish them for having this terminal disease? Obviously that would be absurd! Similarly, we, through no fault of our own, were born infected with the "HIV" of sin. Does God hold resentment toward us for what Adam and Eve did? Would forgiveness make us "well?" Why do *we* need forgiveness?

Forgiveness Removes the Barriers Between God and Us

Now if forgiveness doesn't fix our problem, why does Scripture talk so much about it? Because of guilt. Since we human beings tend to think in terms of imposed rules and imposed penalties, we need the assurance that God doesn't hold anything against us. We need His forgiveness because guilt erects psychological barriers that keep us away from Him. So God, in His typical fashion, meets us where we are, speaks a language we can understand, and gives us a procedure by which the barrier of guilt can be torn down.

A graphic example of this truth is found right after Adam and Eve sinned. When God came to talk to them about it, they were hiding. He knew where they were, but asked, "Where are you?"

In essence they said, "Over here in the bushes. We heard you coming and we were afraid, so we hid." They were afraid to face God because they felt guilty. And because of their guilt, a barrier came between them and God. The barrier was not in God's mind. It was in theirs. *They* were shutting *Him* out, not God shutting them out. And because of this barrier, God could not openly communicate with them. He could not develop a trusting, saving relationship with them. So as a means of removing this barrier, He gave them the concept and procedure of forgiveness, the promise of restoration, and the visual aid of a rite to drive the message home.

We Experience This Barrier in Human Relationships

Those of us who have wronged someone have experienced the barrier that guilt can create. Instead of a free and open relationship, we avoid that person because we feel guilty. We fear what they might be thinking or what they might do or say. This is true even when the other party *doesn't* hold anything against us. Until we ask for, and receive the assurance of their forgiveness, the guilt barrier still stands strong in our minds.

I learned this from experience when one of our daughters was about twelve. Coming home from work one afternoon, my wife and

I found the huge cabinet that formerly hung above the kitchen counter face down in the middle of the floor. I don't remember how many dishes survived, but it was a sight we didn't want to behold. VJ had climbed up to get something out of the cabinet and the whole thing had come crashing down around her. Fortunately she was able to jump clear and escaped injury. But, convinced in her own mind that we would be angry and hold this against her, she ran off and hid in the woods behind our house. We learned of her whereabouts from her brother, and through him, acting as an intermediary, we were finally able to coax her home. But it was not until she repeatedly received messages of forgiveness—messages of assurance that we didn't hold it against her—that the relationship returned to normal.

God Doesn't Hold Anything Against Us

God is forgiveness personified. He doesn't get angry or take offense as humans do, nor does He hold grudges. Jesus didn't hold anything against Peter when he denied him, and He didn't hold anything against Judas, even though Judas betrayed him. Instead of producing anger, antagonism, or resentment in the heart of Jesus, these actions produced hurt, sadness, pity, and love for the perpetrator. God doesn't retaliate, seek revenge, or "get even" for any action against Him. In fact, He can't. These things are foreign to His nature.

But what about those scriptures that seem to indicate otherwise? How do we explain them? It's an old saying, but nevertheless it's true: "It's not what the Bible says, but what it means." As mentioned earlier, God does not speak to us in some elevated heavenly language. He speaks to us in a language and manner we can understand, a language consistent with the culture and context of the day. Unfortunately, when not quoted directly, the words used are those of a human being who is trying to get a message across to imperfect people. The strong words sometimes used are not an accurate reflection of a divine attribute. They are simply stating things in human terms. The devil takes advantage of this and twists the meaning of the words to put his own attributes on God.

I think we would all agree that when things go wrong between two human beings barriers go up in the relationship. But in our relationship with God, the only barrier that ever comes between Him and us is in our own minds because of Satan's lies.

You may have seen the bumper sticker that reads, "Christians aren't perfect, just forgiven." The deeper truth is that God has "forgiven" everyone–if you want to use the term. Some just don't know it, haven't accepted it, or choose to reject it. And in the end, even those who are lost will have been forgiven. They simply didn't choose to take God at His word and listen to what He had to say. How do I know this to be true? Look at Jesus forgiving those who killed Him; they didn't ask for forgiveness. Then why ask? Because when we sincerely ask for forgiveness and trust in His goodness–trusting that He does forgive–the barriers come down and we are put in right relation to God. Receiving God's forgiveness puts us in an attitude of listening to what He has to say to us. Only then can He communicate with us and do for us that which He cannot otherwise do.

When I was a boy, 1 John 1:8 and 9 were very precious to me. When I did something wrong, I knew that if I confessed my sins, God would forgive. And it's true. But the deeper meaning is that God doesn't hold anything against us in the first place. He just wants us to recognize our wrongful acts for what they are, repent of them, and acknowledge our condition and our need. Otherwise He can't help us. J. B. Phillips translates the above passage this way: "If we refuse to admit that we are sinners, then we live in a world of illusion and truth becomes a stranger to us. But if we freely admit that we have sinned, we find God utterly reliable and straightforward–he forgives our sins and makes us thoroughly clean from all that is evil. For if we take up the attitude 'we have not sinned,' we flatly deny God's diagnosis of our condition and cut ourselves off from what he has to say to us" (1 John 1:8–10).

Satan would have us believe that God holds resentment against us, and that somehow His wrath must be quelled in order for us to be saved or even enter into a relationship with Him. But God has provided ample evidence to disprove Satan's lie. Not by claims or statements, but by how Christ treated sinful human beings while He was here on earth.

In a sense God's forgiveness means (to us) just what we always thought it meant, except that it's not something He chooses to extend or withhold like we humans do. His forgiveness is always there. And we especially need it when we *think* He holds something against us.

God's forgiveness is a concept that He has given us to penetrate our rebellious attitudes, remove the barrier of guilt that keeps us away from Him, and restore or establish a saving relationship with Him. So do we need forgiveness when we disobey? Perhaps that will come clear as we look at our next chapter.

Chapter 7
OBEDIENCE

Some people have strong, negative reactions to this word. When they hear it in the context of religion it makes the hair on the back of their necks rise in rebellion. It's like Pavlov's dog salivating at the ringing of a bell. Obviously they've had a bad experience with it somewhere along the line.

Webster says that obedience is "the act or instance of obeying" and obeying means, "to follow the commands or guidance of another." So, to obey God would mean to follow what He has commanded. God has commanded Ten Things, and when these commands are viewed as imposed rules, some conclude that to obey would be legalism. So they reject anything that even smells like obedience. Others believe they're *forced* to do as commanded. "Obey the rules—or else." So they grit their teeth and try to obey—externally.

Generally when we're told we *have to* do something, or we *can't* do something, our natural reaction is to rebel, if not visibly on the outside, then on the inside. We just don't want to be forced to do, or not do anything. It's like the toddler who innocently stood up on the tray of her highchair. After repeated entreaties to sit down went unheeded, Mom finally commanded, "SIT DOWN!" and physically sat her down.

Not to be controlled against her will, the little one responded, "Still standin' up inside!" Sooner or later, forced obedience develops a rebellious character.

Is God trying to force us to obey? We know that the sum and substance of the Ten Commandments is to love God and to love one another, and if one believes that they are just rules, then it follows that God is trying to force us to love Him and everyone else. But love can't be commanded into existence. No one can become loving just because they're told to, even if they have a gun to their head. Besides, we were born with unloving natures, so what does God want of us?

Why Do We Do What We Do?

Of course God is concerned about what we do or don't do, but I believe He is more concerned with our motives—*why* we do or don't do something. For the most part, whether in relation to God's law or man's rules, we obey for one of the following reasons. (It could be for a combination of reasons, but one reason usually dominates.)

1. We want to avoid the penalty for disobedience.
2. We are trying to please. Because (a) we feel obligated, and/or (b) we love someone and want to make him or her happy.
3. We've been trained to do or not to do something.
4. We understand the issues at hand and see that a certain course of action is the best or right thing to do. We agree and do what's right just because it *is* right.

In religion, if we think the law is imposed rules, it's easy to be motivated by the first or second reason. If number one is my reason, the logic is: God has commanded it, He is Sovereign, and He has the power to reward or destroy. I don't want to get in trouble with Him, so out of fear of what He will do to me I try to obey the rules. The logic behind number 2(a) goes something like this: I am under the condemnation of the law but Christ has taken my punishment so I'm off the hook. Therefore I'm in His debt and *obligated* to do what He wants. (This can get to be *heavy* obligation—and guilt too, if I think I might not be obeying well enough.) If 2(b) is my reason, I want to please Him because I love Him for what He has done for me. He took my place and died for my sins. He took my punishment and paid the penalty that was mine. This differs from 2a in that now I'm *genuinely* grateful and *really do* love Him. Now please don't misunderstand.

We have good reason to be grateful for what Christ has done for us and I don't want to minimize this in the least. Christ said, "If ye love me, keep my commandments" (John 14:15, KJV). So it's understandable that many believe that obedience for reason 2(b) is what God wants. And it *is* what God wants if that's where we are on our journey to a mature relationship with God. But I believe this is not the mature motivation God ultimately wants.

When we were kids we generally obeyed for reasons one and two. (Hopefully not 2(a) because this is really not a healthy reason for anyone to obey, especially adults.) We had to be told to wash our hands before eating. It was a rule. So we did it because we didn't want to get in trouble with the one who made the rule. If we did it at all, we started out it doing out of fear of what would happen to us if we didn't. And as we grew older we may have done it to please Mom or Dad. But when we became adults, hopefully we matured enough to do or not do things for better reasons. If so, somewhere along the way we began to understand *why* we should do it, and we decided we wanted to do it, because it made good sense. We "obeyed" and washed our hands because *we* chose to do it of our own free will. It was just the right thing to do if we didn't want to eat germs and get sick.

Because the commandments to love are inextricably linked to the descriptive moral law in cause-effect relationship, obedience for reasons numbers one and two ultimately doesn't make any sense. For example, do you relate to the law of gravity the way you do because you're afraid of what God will do to you, because you feel obligated to Him, or because you are trying to please Him? Of course not. But because many believe God's law is just rules, these are the very reasons for their obedience—whether they realize it or not.

Ultimately, the example about washing our hands is how God wants adult Christians to relate to what He has told us to do. Though we may start out being motivated by fear, obligation, or wanting to please, God wants us to "grow up" and do what we do or don't do for mature reasons, because we have thought it through and act from an intelligent understanding of cause and effect. Yes, we're humans and our natures don't naturally love in a mature way. But when we see God as the kind of person He really is; when we understand that the true nature of the law is fixed; that love is the foundation of His government—the way He runs His universe; when we realize that love must abound in order for there to be peace, order, and harmony all around; when we see the wisdom of God's ways, "buy into" His program and want our thoughts, emotions, feelings, motives, desires (and of course our behavior) to be totally loving; when we see all this, doesn't it makes good sense to choose to think and act in loving ways as best we can even if we're not completely changed on the inside yet? Not to earn anything, but because of the benefit to everyone involved? Ourselves included? "The law always ended up being used as a Band-Aid on sin instead of a deep healing of it. And now what the law code asked for but we couldn't deliver is accomplished as we, instead of redoubling our own efforts, simply embrace what the Spirit is doing in us" (Rom. 8:3, 4, MSG).

True "Obedience"

So obedience, if we must use the term, is a willingness to listen to what God has to say to us, agreeing with it and embracing it; it means seeking to be in harmony with the principle of love and acting in ways that produce peace and unity. "You will be doing the right thing if you obey the law of the Kingdom, which is found in the scripture, 'Love your neighbor as you love yourself'" (James 2:8, GNB).

So, *"obedience" is simply loving*. But it's more than performing external acts of love, although it certainly includes this. It involves the enthusiastic embracing of God's program, and having an attitude of wanting to be made loving on the inside. It means saying yes to God's Spirit—the Spirit of truth and love.

So, "accept the word that he plants in your heart, which is able to save you" (James 1:21, GNB). "For it is God Himself whose power creates within you the desire to do His gracious will and also brings about the accomplishment of the desire" (Phil. 2:13, WNT).

Chapter 8
PERFECTION

Perfection! This subject is so powerful it strikes fear in the hearts of many conscientious Christians and raises the hackles of rebellion in others. In religious circles its connotation is so negative that those friendly to the term are often labeled as legalists. Why? What's the basis for all this negative reaction?

Webster defines "perfection" as "freedom from fault or defect, ... the quality or state of being saintly." And the word "perfect," he says, means "being entirely without fault or defect." So, many conclude that to reach the state of sainthood we must be entirely without fault. We must work on eliminating all our defects. We are to be good by not being bad. And with this conclusion we're right back to imposed rules and legalism. No wonder this word causes so much negative reaction. But is there any Scriptural basis for perfection in the Christian life?

Is Perfection Scriptural?

In Scripture there are many passages that talk about various people being perfect or not being perfect. (Noah–Gen 6:9; David–1 Kings 11:4; Job–Job 1:1; Zachariah and Elizabeth–Luke 1:6; and Nathanael–John 1:47). And Christ Himself admonished us to be perfect. "Be ye therefore perfect," He said, "even as your Father which is in heaven is perfect" (Matt. 5:48, KJV). Ouch! That's pretty plain. We're *commanded* to be perfect. How do we get around that? But what did He mean?

The Context of This Command

Christ was giving the Sermon on the Mount. After going through the Beatitudes, He said, "Do not think that I came to abolish the Law or the Prophets; I did not come to abolish, but to fulfill" (Matt. 5:17, NASB). He wasn't saying He was annulling or doing away with the law. He was saying, "What I say and do is a perfect fulfillment of everything specified in the law." He then tells the people that unless *their* law keeping surpasses that of the Pharisees and teachers of the law, they will not enter the kingdom of heaven. He contrasts what these teachers taught about anger, adultery, promises, and retaliation, with what it really means to "keep" or "fulfill" the law's requirements.

Then He comes to the perfection part. He concludes this portion of His sermon by saying, "You have heard it said 'Thou shalt love thy neighbor and hate thine enemy', but I tell you, Love your enemies, and pray for those who persecute you, so you may be sons of your Heavenly Father. For He makes his sun rise upon evil men as well as good, and sends rain upon honest and dishonest men alike.

"For if you love only those who love you, what credit is that to you? Even tax-collectors do that! And if you exchange greetings only with your own circle, are you doing anything exceptional? Even the pagans do that much. No, you are to be perfect, like your Heavenly Father" (Matt. 5:46–48, Phillips).

Notice that the whole discussion is about love, what they were formerly taught about it, and how they "loved" (or didn't) as opposed to how God loves. Then Christ concludes by referring to what the Pharisees and the teachers of the Law taught and did. In essence He said, "Don't love like they do, that's not genuine love, that's not fulfilling the spirit of the law. Love like your heavenly Father does—love perfectly."

So What Is Perfection?

The original Greek word *teleios*, from which the word "perfect" was translated, means "complete," "full grown," or "mature." Those who love only those who love them, don't have a love that is "full grown" or "mature." Even many who aren't Christians love that way. But God wants our love to be different. He wants it to reach maturity, or perfection, if you please. And *perfection is loving in a spiritually mature, other-centered, grownup way; loving perfectly* from the heart, like God does. Though Christ commanded us to love perfectly, we know (and so does He) that commanding it can't produce love, nor can we make it happen by grit or determination anymore than we can make ourselves grow taller. Sure, we can grit our teeth and go through the motions if we have to, but we know it's not the real thing. So if God wants the genuine stuff, and we can't produce it, what's the solution? We'll deal with that in a later chapter. First, we must look at some other important subjects.

Chapter 9
GRACE

When you think of all the ways we use this word, it's no wonder we have trouble communicating on the subject. We say grace and we're given grace. We can have grace in our hearts and yet we're under grace. It is with us, it is sufficient for us, and it is abundant. We're saved by grace, kept by grace, and transformed by grace. We can frustrate it, hope through it, grow in it, and yet fall from it. It's the only antidote for evil, it comes from God, and it's free. So what is it exactly?

Technical Definitions

Unfortunately the meaning of "grace" has changed over time. As of late, it is equated with pardon. And we certainly don't want to leave that out. My friend and I would have been happy to receive this kind of grace in court. But to limit "grace" to pardon only would be much too narrow. Except for one instance in the King James New Testament (James 1:11), the word "grace" is always translated from the Greek word *charis* (khar'-ece).

Strong's Greek Dictionary of the New Testament defines *charis* as "graciousness ... of manner or act (abstract or concrete; literal, figurative or spiritual; especially the divine influence upon the heart, and its reflection in the life; including gratitude)." In addition to being translated as "grace," the word "*charis*" is also translated in the King James Version as "acceptable," "benefit," "favor," "gift," "gracious," "joy," "liberality," "pleasure," "thank," and "thanks." Are we getting anywhere? Yes, stick with me; we're almost there.

Paraphrasing from *Vine's Expository Dictionary of Biblical Words*, *charis* is something that gives pleasure, delight, or causes favorable regard in the believer. It is applied to the beauty, or graciousness of a person (Luke 2:40), act (2 Cor. 8:6), or of speech (Luke 4:22, RV). It implies a friendly disposition on the part of the person from whom kindly acts proceed, i.e., graciousness, lovingkindness, and goodwill generally (Acts 7:10), especially when it refers to divine favor or "grace" (Acts 14:26). In this respect there is emphasis on its freeness, universal bestowal, and its spontaneous character. Okay, enough of the technical stuff. Let's boil all this down to where we can make sense out of it.

Grace Is God's Graciousness

From all of this three things stand out. (1) Grace is the gracious manner or acts that spontaneously proceed from someone with a gracious, friendly disposition. (2) Grace produces or occasions pleasure or delight in the believer. And (3) grace is reflected in the life of the believer. Is it accurate to say that God has a friendly disposition and spontaneously acts in a gracious manner toward all? Absolutely. Regardless of who we are or how we act, that's always the way He is. That's grace! How do we know this to be true? The evidence is in the attitude and actions as seen in God the Son. Look at what He taught and how He treated others. And He said, "If you have seen Me, you have seen the Father." God is graciousness personified.

Since God is love, does His graciousness spring from His love, or does His love spring from His graciousness? Or are they the same? Because it's possible to *act* graciously without actually being a loving person, we would have to take the position that *genuine* graciousness is the outward manifestation of a love that dwells within. Therefore, even though grace is God's graciousness, the essence of *grace is His uplifting, redeeming love*, freely given, unconditional, steadfast, persistent, and unquenchable. Does this produce or occasion pleasure or delight in the believer? Definitely! And is it reflected in the life of the true believer? Without a doubt! Therefore, it can be stated that God's grace is revealed by His unconditional love toward sinners.

Chapter 10
FAITH

Many have an erroneous idea of what faith is. Mark Twain once said faith was "believing what you know ain't so." Elbert Hubbard believed that faith was "the effort to believe what your common sense tells you is not true." And Zlatko said, "If the Lord had meant us to have faith, he'd have given us lobotomies." And from the pulpit the following story is often told to illustrate what faith looks like. It goes something like this:

The crowd excitedly jockeys for best position at the viewpoint overlooking Niagara Falls. Everyone is eager to see the aerialist who boasts he will walk a tight wire strung across the falls. At the appointed time a man with a long pole appears on the platform. Carefully, as if to test it, he places his foot on the wire, then cautiously begins the daring and dangerous feat. What courage! What skill! Breathlessly the crowd watch as the stunt man carefully negotiates his way to a point directly over the most dangerous part of the falls and stops. Now what? To the crowd's amazement he jumps in the air, turns and comes down facing the other way, then proceeds back to the starting point.

The crowd roars its admiration and approval, and then quiets as they see a wheelbarrow lifted to the platform. The acrobat places it on the wire, turns to the crowd and begins to speak. "Do you think I can wheel this across?"

"Yes," shouts the enthusiastic crowd.

"Are you sure I can do it?" he queries.

"Yes," roars the crowd.

Addressing an especially enthusiastic spectator who just arrived on the scene, the tightrope walker puts the question to him directly. Do you believe I can wheel this across?"

"Yes," says the man.

"Do you have faith in me that I can do it?" asks the wirewalker.

"Yes, go for it," replies the man without hesitation.

"OK," says the acrobat, "if you really believe I can, get in the wheelbarrow."

Faith or Presumption?

Now, if the man gets in, is he showing genuine faith? What evidence does the spectator have that the tightrope walker can do it? If he has no evidence and he got in the wheelbarrow, it would not be a show of faith. It would be presumption. Presumption because he is *presuming* the man can do it—belief without evidence.

But as Thomas H. Huxley said, "The deepest sin against the human mind is to believe things without evidence." Unfortunately, thousands have this kind of faith. It's called "blind faith," and many, along with David Keating tout it as a great Christian virtue. Keating said, "Blind faith is the bedrock upon which all of our belief systems are built. It is the starting point for each individual journey ... So let us celebrate our blind faith, as unprovable as it is unshakable. For without it, we would have no faith at all." But this kind of faith is not faith. It is presumption, and it is the devil's counterfeit.

Faith or Make Believe?

Others have a different kind of "faith." It's similar to Elbert Hubbard's brand. It's like "if you believe hard enough, it will come true." Some years ago the sailboat on which three people were crossing the Pacific Ocean overturned in a storm. Weary days and nights passed as they hoped against hope and clung to the remains of their craft. One, a Christian, had more to cling to. He had his faith. He prayed and prayed, and told the others he had faith they all would be rescued. He got to the point of believing it with all his heart. Eventually help did come, but too late. Only one lived to tell the story, and it wasn't the Christian. Many, when praying for healing, fall into the trap of this kind of "faith." And when healing doesn't come it is either attributed to a lack of faith, or their "faith" is destroyed.

What Is Genuine Faith?

Though many stories have been told, thousands of sermons preached, and hundreds of books written on the subject, yet to many, faith remains vague, misunderstood and misapplied. And the old standby definition from Hebrews 11:1 in the King James apparently hasn't helped us much either. In fact, it seems to support the "faith" we've just been discussing: "Now faith is the substance of things hoped for, the evidence of things not seen." But this verse is really not defining what faith *is*. It's describing what faith *does*. The New English Bible reads this way: "And what is faith? Faith gives assurance to our hopes, and makes us certain of realities we do not see" margin. But the assurance and the certainty still have to be based on evidence.

Aside from referring to our religious belief as "our faith," faith is really something we *do*. In Scripture, the original Greek word *pistis* is generally translated "faith." It's a verb rather than a noun. Now since faith is something active, rather than passive, a better translation would be the synonym "trust." And it *is* rendered "trust" in many modern translations. It's also how we use the word "faith" in everyday conversation. Oddly we don't seem to have any trouble with its meaning in this context. If a bridge is considered unsafe, we won't cross it because we don't have faith in its ability to hold us up. What we mean is, we don't trust it. Now if we did trust it, we wouldn't say "I faith the bridge" because that would be grammatically incorrect. We would say, "I *trust* the bridge," meaning, "I believe in the bridge's ability to hold us up." That's proper, and it's easier to understand.

Perhaps one reason for the difficulty is that the only way to properly use "faith" as a verb, is to use it in its transitive form: "I have faith *in* the bridge." The word "faith" must have an object. And just as the *word* "faith" must have an object, so it is with faith itself. Having or possessing faith isn't faith unless we put it *in* something or someone. Using the word "trust" seems to overcome these difficulties because it can be used either way.

So, if we have faith in a person, it means we believe in, or trust that person. And in order to trust someone, we must know them well, and have evidence that they can be trusted. Generally, we don't trust anyone unless they first show themselves to be trustworthy—unless you're foolish like the followers of Jim Jones or David Koresh. Their followers had "faith" in them without any evidence they could be trusted. And as far as I know, their followers didn't even ask any questions. They just did whatever they were told. Talk about "blind faith!" And you know where it got them. Dead.

God Wants Intelligent Faith

But God doesn't want "blind faith." He wants us to have intelligent faith. He gave us a brain so we could think, reason, and do like He does, and He expects us to use it. He wants us to ask questions so He can lead us to the answers. God wants our faith to be based on evidence. Then when He says things like, "I forgive you," we'll believe (trust) Him. And when He asks us to do this, or don't do that, we'll trust that He has our best interests in mind. But in order to trust—have genuine faith in—God, we must come to know Him as the trustworthy person He really is.

How Do We Get to Know Him?

But how can we know God? First, Scripture says, "what may be known about God is plain ... because God has made it plain ... For since the creation of the world God's invisible qualities—his eternal power and divine nature—have been clearly seen, being understood from what has been made, so that men are without excuse" (Rom 1:19, 20, NIV). Secondly, we also get to know God through the study of His Word. The Bible is not meant to be a codebook of rules and regulations to follow, nor is it meant to be studied as literature, although it is certainly that. Our study of Scripture should be with one purpose in mind—to get to know God. Christ said, "You study the Scriptures diligently because you think that in them you have eternal life." But "these are the very Scriptures that testify about me" (John 5:39, NIV).

As we study, we should ask such questions as, "What does this tell me about God?" "What kind of person is He?" "Why would He say or do this?" "Can I believe what He says?" "Is He trustworthy?" "How do I know?" "What evidence do I have that this is so?" "Does He have my best interest in mind?" "What does this tell me about how He relates to and interacts with the people He has created?" And when He does or says something we don't understand, it's OK to ask "why?" Although it's not ordinarily thought of in this way, this approach is real theology. It's theology because the word "theology" means the study of God.

What Faith Means

So to have faith in God means to believe, or trust Him. And He does not ask us to believe without giving adequate evidence on which to base our faith. In other words, God wants our faith, belief, or trust (all synonyms) to be rooted in evidence, not presumption. Of course He wants us to believe that He is the way He says He is, and that He will do what He says He will do. *But not just because He said it.* Anyone can make claims. He wants us to believe Him because we have been convinced by the evidence that He *can* be trusted. Genuine *faith* is simply *trust*. And when it comes to a human being or God, trust is the firm reliance on the integrity, ability, or character of someone. Put another way, *true faith is having an intelligent confidence in God based on evidence.* Instead of some commodity we possess, it's something we do. And it's the only basis for a saving relationship with God.

Chapter 11
SALVATION

To some, salvation is merely a legal transaction that gives them a ticket to heaven and an escape from hell. But given the true nature of the law and our condition, a judicial act can no more fix our problem than it can fix someone with AIDS.

According to Webster, the word "salvation" means "deliverance." And looking back at the original Greek word, *soteria*, from which the word "salvation" was translated, we find that "deliverance" is indeed the original meaning. So nothing has changed in terms of the meaning of the word itself. But the question is, deliverance from what? In court, my friend and I wanted deliverance from imposed punishment. Is this the way it is in Christianity? If the law were imposed rules it would be. In this frame of reference who wouldn't want to be delivered from suffering an imposed penalty for breaking God's rules? But let's go back and let Webster finish his definition. He says "salvation" means "deliverance from the *power* and *effects* of sin" (emphasis mine). Is he right?

What Did Christ Teach About This?

Shortly after Christ began His ministry in Galilee, He visited His home church in Nazareth. When they asked Him to read the Scripture, He read a familiar passage from the book of Isaiah, which was commonly understood to refer to the coming Messiah. "The Spirit of the Lord is on me," He said, "because he hath anointed me to preach the gospel to the poor; he hath sent me to heal the brokenhearted, to preach deliverance to the captives, and recovering of sight to the blind, to set at liberty them that are bruised." He then finished by saying, "This day is this scripture fulfilled in your ears" (Luke 4:18, 21, KJV).

With this statement Christ was proclaiming Himself to be the Messiah. And the passage He read describes the Messiah's work as being about deliverance, liberty, and healing. But the question remains, what is involved in this deliverance, liberty, and healing?

The apostle Paul says, "Scripture declares that the whole world is a *prisoner* of sin" (Gal. 3:22, NIV, emphasis mine). And, "that, though you used to be *slaves* to sin ... you have been *set free*" (Rom. 6:17, 18, NIV, emphasis mine). When John the Baptist saw Jesus he said, "Behold the Lamb of God, which *taketh away the sin* of the world" (John 1:29, KJV, emphasis mine). Salvation, then, is all about being delivered and freed, not only from the penalty of sin, but delivered, freed, and healed from the captivity, blindness, and oppression of sin. Because the Jews only wanted a Messiah who would deliver them from the Romans, they missed the true meaning of the Messiah's work. Consequently they didn't accept Him when He came.

Practically Speaking, What Does This Mean?

Notice salvation has several aspects. In order for it to be complete, it must include all of these. First, Christ, the Light of the world, came to deliver us from the blindness of our sinful natures, to illuminate our minds so we can "see" our condition, realize our need, and discern spiritual things.

He said, "'For judgment I have come into this world, so that the blind will see and those who see will become blind.' Then some of the Pharisees who were with Him heard these words, and said to Him, 'Are we blind also?' Jesus said to them, 'If you were blind, you would have no sin; but now you say, "We see." Therefore your sin remains'" (John 9:39–41, NIV). Because these Pharisees weren't willing to "see" or admit their condition, Christ couldn't help them.

Speaking of them Christ told His disciples, "For this people's heart has become calloused; they hardly hear with their ears, and they have closed their eyes. Otherwise they might see with their eyes, hear with their ears, understand with their hearts and turn, and I would heal them" (Matt. 13:15, NIV).

Unfortunately, we all suffer from this "blindness." And deliverance is only possible if we're willing to "see" or acknowledge our condition and our need. That's why Christ's admonition to the Laodicean church is "I counsel thee to ... anoint thine eyes with eye salve, that thou mayest see" (Rev. 3:18, KJV).

Second, God wants to deliver us from guilt. Not guilt in a legal sense, but what we feel inside. Guilt is one of the most oppressive and imprisoning things we human beings can experience. It can eat out the very core of one's life. Salvation includes being freed from the prison house of guilt. And yes, if in our understanding we are thinking in a legal mode, He will take care of that too.

Third, salvation includes deliverance from the power that sin has over us. We think, speak, act, and react the way we do because, like the scorpion, it's our nature, and we're in bondage to it. Paul realized this when he said, "For I know that good itself does not dwell in me, that is, in my sinful nature ... For I do not do the good I want to do, but the evil I do not want to do–this I keep on doing ... What a wretched man I am! Who will rescue me from this body that is subject to death? Thanks be to God, who delivers me through Jesus Christ our Lord!" (Rom 7:18–25, NIV)

And Jesus said, "if the Son sets you *free*, you will be *free* indeed" (John 8:36, NIV, emphasis mine). So part of the package is deliverance from our selfish, unloving nature. Sadly, some like sin and don't want to be saved from its power.

Fourth, since we are all held hostage by Satan on this sin-saturated planet, salvation must also include the ultimate deliverance from this captivity. That is, it must include deliverance from the presence of sin. And when Christ physically rescues us from this earth, we will be forever free from sin in all its aspects.

So, since the moral law is a fixed one, and we are "sick in the head," salvation means to be (1) healed of the blindness that prevents us from seeing our condition (John 9:39); (2) freed from guilt (1 John 1:8–10); (3) healed of our unloving and destructive desires, motives, inclinations, feelings, and emotions, and what they make us think and do (Jer. 31:31-33); (4) freed from the ultimate consequences of remaining in this condition; and (5) delivered from the presence of everything that is at odds with God's law by physically rescuing us from this world (John 14:3).

In short, accepting God's *salvation means to be saved from the blindness, guilt, power, consequences, and presence of sin*. It's a package deal. We don't have the option to pick and choose here. We must agree to all aspects or we get the benefits of none. I've heard people say they can remember the very day they "got saved." But, assuming they were sincere, on that day they only experienced the first and second benefits of salvation. In order to experience salvation, in the end, we must stay with Christ. He said, "Remain united to me, and I will remain united to you ... Those who do not remain in me are thrown out like a branch and dry up; such branches are gathered up and thrown into the fire, where they are burned" (John 15:4, 6, GNB).

Salvation means healing and restoration. God wants to heal us from the sickness of sin and restore us to the original condition that Adam and Eve enjoyed before their fall. And praise God; "All this is done by God, who through Christ changed us from enemies into his friends" (2 Cor. 5:18, GNB).

Chapter 12
JUSTIFICATION

After hearing the preacher's sermon, and knowing he was to speak again that afternoon, a young girl asked someone, "Will you please ask the minister to speak easy words that we can understand? Will you please tell him we do not understand large words, like justification and sanctification?" Though one might not expect someone of her age to understand "justification," I've found that many adults don't seem to know what it actually means either, or how it works.

Justification Is Getting Set Right

According to Webster, "justification" is "the act, process, or state of being justified." But that doesn't help much unless we know what "justified" means. "Justified" is the past tense of the verb "to justify"; and "to justify" means "to make just" or "to make right." So, in plain English, "justification" *is the action of making, putting, or setting us right.* These are Webster's definitions of these English words, but one can see from the table below that the meaning of the words from which they were translated have the same meaning.

Greek Word	Original Meaning	King James Version	Word Form
dikaioo	to make, set, or put right	justify	verb
dikaioo	already made, set, or put right	justified	verb (past tense)

Greek Word	Original Meaning	King James Version	Word Form
dikaiosis	process, or act of being put right	justification	noun
dikaioma	a deed or act that is shown to be right	justification	noun

Notice the meanings of all these words all have to do with "right." But "right" must be in relation to something or somebody. And of course, in this case we are talking about being right with, or in right relation to, God.

What Does It Take to be Right With God?

How does justification happen? What does it look like? Is it a judicial decision in the Supreme Court of the Universe? Is it an accounting transaction in the Accounts Receivable Department in the Heavenly Government Accounting Office so that all debts are accounted as paid in full? What does it take to be right with God? What is the issue? Scripture uses many metaphors to help us understand justification. But these metaphors, given to a specific people in a specific culture, are just that—metaphors. They are not the real thing. They were simply meant to illustrate and help us understand the meaning of the real thing. Unfortunately, though, too often we get stuck on the metaphors and never get past them to the objective reality.

The reality is, that being right with God is relationship oriented, and it works much the same as it does between human beings. In human relationships, when two parties are in right relation to each other—as in a good marriage or friendship—there is love, peace, trust, harmony, and good communication. Things are right between them. When things go wrong, barriers arise, and the relationship is not restored until things are right between the parties. So far, this is exactly how it works in our relationship with God.

But here's where the similarity ends. In human relationships either party can wrong the other, and either one can become offended or rebellious and pull away. But this is not the case in our relationship with God. We can wrong Him, but *He* never wrongs *us*. He is always faithful, fair, and true (Rom. 3:4; 2 Tim. 2:13; Rev. 15:3; 19:11). Furthermore, He never becomes offended by what we say or do. His attitude toward us never changes, *no matter what*. How do we know this to be true? When God the Son was being tortured and killed was He offended or angry with His murderers? No, He prayed, "Father, forgive them; for they know not what they do" (Luke 23:34, KJV).

When Adam and Eve chose another to be their god, God wasn't offended or angry, nor did He pull away. He was sad. Very sad. When He asked Adam and Eve where they were, they admitted that they were hiding because they were afraid. Why were they afraid? In reality they had no reason to be afraid. Nevertheless their fear was real because *they believed the lies* Satan had told them about God. The problem was in *their* minds. So instead of leaving them to reap the inevitable consequence of their choice, God in His graciousness pursued them and brought them back into right relation with Himself. How did He do this? Somehow He convinced them that He was not angry with them, that there was no need to be afraid, and that He loved them and still wanted a relationship with them. And when they believed, or trusted God, they were set right with Him.

It's the same with us. The apostle Paul says, we are set right with God "through personal faith [or by trusting] in Jesus Christ." He goes on to say that "we believed in Jesus as the Messiah so that we might be set right before God by trusting in the Messiah" (Gal. 2:16, MSG). So we are set right with God by trusting or believing in Jesus Christ.

Paul explains how this works by citing Abraham's experience: "He believed God, and that act of belief was turned into a life that was right with God" (Gal. 3:6, MSG). What did Abraham believe? He believed what God told him. And Moses wrote that "Abram believed the

Lord, and the Lord was pleased with him" (Gen. 15:6, CEV). In other words, Abraham believed and trusted God, and because this is what it takes, God announced that Abraham was in right relation to Him.

In the story about the Pharisee and the tax collector, Jesus contrasts how one *doesn't* become right with God with what it really takes *to* become right with Him.

"The Pharisee," Jesus said, "stood by himself and prayed: 'God, I thank you that I am not like other people—robbers, evildoers, adulterers—or even like this tax collector. I fast twice a week and give a tenth of all I get.' But the tax collector stood at a distance. He would not even look up to heaven, but beat his breast and said, 'God, have mercy on me, a sinner.'" Then Jesus said, "I tell you that this man, rather than the other, went home justified [set right] before God" (Luke 18:11–14, NIV, emphasis mine). Why was this man set right with God and not the Pharisee? Because, unlike the Pharisee, the tax collector (1) realized his condition and his need; and (2) he believed God, and trusted in His goodness and power to save. The Pharisee felt no need, and instead of believing God and trusting in His goodness, his trust was in his own so-called goodness.

Our God is a friendly God. All He wants is a harmonious, loving, trusting relationship with us. But it can't happen unless all the barriers are removed, and everything is right between us. When we realize our condition and need, when the Holy Spirit takes the truth about God's loving character and opens it to our understanding, then we begin to see God as He truly is. When we are convinced of His incredible, unconditional love, acceptance, mercy and forgiveness, and respond and believe (or trust) what He says, we are put in right relation with Him. *Justification is being set right with God in the attitude of our minds.* It happens when the Holy Spirit reveals the truth about God to us and we respond by believing (trusting) Him.

Chapter 13
RIGHTEOUSNESS

Ask a group of people to define what "righteousness" actually is and you will no doubt get a lot of blank stares. I've discovered that to most it seems vague and intangible; something they can't quite put their finger on. No wonder. The way we refer to it, it could either be some kind of commodity, something we put on, an entry in the Heavenly General Ledger, or a judicial decision. Furthermore, we are admonished to awake to it, be instructed in it, seek it, hunger and thirst for it, follow after it, and live for it. We're promised to be covered with it, filled with it, have it imputed to us, perfected in us, and given a crown of it. Consequently, we debate whether it happens to us, on us, in us, or about us. One thing most Christians agree on, though: it's not a do-it-yourself project. We know the Jews tried that method and failed miserably.

Though many may be unsure of what righteousness actually is, the meaning in Scripture, according to the English, Greek, and Hebrew dictionaries, hasn't changed from when this word was originally translated. "Righteousness" in the New Testament, originally spelled "rightwiseness," is most often translated from the Greek word *dikaiosune* (dik-ah-yos-oo'-nay). *Dikaiosune* comes from the word *dikaios*, which comes from the word "dike," which means, "right." The adjective form of the word "right" is "righteous," and "righteousness" is the noun form of the word. The Greek word *dikaiosune* and its English counterpart, "righteousness," still mean "being, or acting in a right, or 'rightwise' manner." OK. Enough of that. In everyday English, what does it mean to be "rightwise" and act in a "rightwise" manner?

To be "Rightwise" Means to be Like God

Since God is righteous, He is the only true standard of "rightwiseness" or righteousness. Therefore, to be righteous would mean to be like God. What is God like? "God is love" (1 John 4:16). King David said, "All thy commandments are righteousness" (Ps. 119:172, KJV). In agreement with that, James points out that "if you really keep the royal law found in Scripture, 'Love your neighbor as yourself,' you are doing right [acting righteously]" (James 2:8, NIV). So, since God is love, and love is also the fulfilling of the law (Rom. 13:10), to be righteous is to be loving. In essence then, love is righteousness. Therefore *righteousness is love*.

But what about when God *declares* someone righteous? What does that mean? When God declares something it means He makes it known. When He declares His own righteousness He declares it by what He does (Rom. 3:25). It's not just a claim. He makes it apparent by what he does, by demonstrating that He always does the right thing, the loving thing. God is totally righteous. He loves perfectly. It's His nature. But our nature is just the opposite of God's. We're unrighteous—selfish in nature. Our loving, our righteousness, is as filthy rags. So how can God declare a person as righteous when they're not? He is simply making known what He knows about that person. Of course He knows that we don't have a righteous character like Adam and Eve did before the fall but He is simply declaring that the person's heart is right with Him. He is saying that because the person has bought into His program, has a willingness to listen, and is allowing Him to work in him "both to will and to do of his good pleasure" (Phil. 2:13), that the person is on the right track to love. The person is in right relationship with God. And when Scripture says that God *accounts* someone righteous it's the same. If the person is truly in right relationship with God, He knows, and He can announce or account that person as righteous. And it will also show in that person's life.

Chapter 14
JUSTICE

"People don't want to hear about the other side of God," the preacher began. "They get uncomfortable and don't want to talk about it."

Is he serious? I pondered. Or was this a clever attempt to get my attention? Curious, I listened up.

"We know God is loving, but He *does* have this other side," he continued. He *was* serious, and now I was *really* listening. He went on to cite various examples in Scripture of judgments imposed on wicked people. Then, to drive the message home, he ended up with what God will do to sin and sinners in the end.

Does God have this other side? Many Christians believe He does. "God is not only loving," they say, "but He's also just." What they mean is that inside God's velvet glove of love, is an iron fist of vengeance and retribution for those who don't love Him and do what He says. They call it "justice."

"Justice" is another of those words whose meaning has changed over time. In the English language it used to mean the maintenance or administration of law in a right, impartial, fair, or equitable manner. And those who were impartial and fair in all their dealings, acted in harmony with the principle of justice. But now, the use and meaning of this word—though not yet defined this way in the dictionaries—has come to be almost exclusively punitive. When convicted criminals are executed for their crimes we say, "justice has been done." But it is rare that we say this about someone charged with a crime and acquitted when they were really innocent.

This drift in meaning has now found its way into some versions of Scripture. In the past the Hebrew word, *tsedeq* (tseh'-dek), and the

Greek word *dikaiosune* (dik-ah-yos-oo'-nay), were more often translated as "righteousness." But now, in some modern versions, both of these original words are often translated as "justice." Sometimes the difference is from version to version, but sometimes it's within the same version. This would not be so much of a problem if the original meaning of "acting in a fair and impartial manner" were applied. But the connotation is clearly punitive.

For example, in Romans 3:21–26, in the King James, New Revised Standard, and the November 1978 second printing of The New International Version, we find the Greek word *dikaiosune* is translated "righteousness" in all cases except for verses 25 and 26 in the NIV, which translates it as "justice." Here's how they read (emphasis mine):

- KJV: "Whom God hath set forth to be a propitiation through faith in his blood, *to declare his righteousness* for the remission of sins that are past, through the forbearance of God" (verse 25). "*To declare*, I say, at this time *his righteousness*: that he might be just, and the justifier of him which believeth in Jesus" (verse 26).

- NRSV: "Whom God put forward as a sacrifice of atonement by his blood, effective through faith. He did this *to show his righteousness*, because in his divine forbearance he had passed over the sins previously committed" (verse 25). "It was *to prove* at the present time *that he himself is righteous* and that he justifies the one who has faith in Jesus" (verse 26).

- NIV: "God presented him as a sacrifice of atonement, through faith in his blood. He did this *to demonstrate his justice,* because in his forbearance he had left the sins committed beforehand unpunished" (verse 25). "He did it *to demonstrate his justice* at the present time, so as to be just and the one who justifies those who have faith in Jesus" (verse 26).

Why would the translators of the original edition of the NIV choose the word righteousness in verses 21 and 22, and "justice" in verses 25 and 26? Since they are all translated from the same Greek word *dikaiosune*, why not always translate it as "righteousness?" Could it be that the translators thought "justice" conveyed the negative connotation of vengeance, retribution and imposed punishment they thought was called for in the context? But why would they think that? Perhaps it was because of their personal frame of reference. If they perceived the law as imposed rules, it would be natural for them to believe that God has to impose punishment—mete out "justice" for breaking the rules. Perhaps in their minds God is like Nebuchadnezzar, who says "bow down and worship me, or I'll mete out justice by throwing you into the burning fiery furnace."

However, in all fairness to the NIV translators, it should be noted that the 2011 version corrects this and uses the word "righteousness" instead of "justice," as used in the 1978 version.

It is interesting to note that the word "justice" is not found in the New Testament in the King James Version Bible; it appears only in the Old Testament. And except for one text in Job, it is always translated from the Hebrew word *tsadaq* (tsaw-dak'), which means to "be, or make right," or from two other forms of this word: *tsedeq,* "the right," and *tsedaqaqah,* "rightness."

The point is that, whether in the Old or New Testament, whatever the version, the words translated "justice" and "righteousness" are from the same word. There is no connotation of vengeance, retribution, or any kind of imposed punishment in the original meanings. They simply have to do with fairness, impartiality, equity, and rightness.

Since righteousness is love, and "to justify" means "to put right," and to have faith in someone is to trust them, permit me to go back to the above passage in Romans and insert the words "love" or "loving" in place of "righteousness" and "righteous." Let's also substitute "puts right" in place of "justifies," and put "trust" in place of the word "faith." In plain English then, both the KJV and the NRSV would read, "He did this to show His love" and "it was to prove that He is loving, and that He puts right those who trust in Jesus." No connotation of vengeance or retribution.

Is God not only loving but also just? Well, yes, but it's like saying, "God is not only loving, but He is also fair, equitable, and impartial." It's all the same because that's the way love is. Being just is not the other side of God. He doesn't have another side.

So what does "justice" mean? When it's used about God in the proper way, it means moral or absolute rightness. It means He maintains and administers the natural laws of the universe and deals with us in an honorable, upright, and impartial way. A just way. It means He doesn't alter or do away with these laws for any reason— ever. They are forever fixed. And because the moral law is also fixed, God doesn't change or do away with this law either. Not even to save sinners. That's why we need a Savior. But if we do not let God heal and restore us, He will reluctantly permit us to experience the natural consequences of relating to the fixed moral law in a manner that brings serious negative consequences. Webster says justice is the quality of being just, impartial, or fair ... the principle ... of just dealing or right action. And I think Webster's right. Pun intended.

Chapter 15
WORKS

I used to have a lot of conversations with myself about works. They went something like this: "Am I saved by faith?"
"Yes."
"By faith alone?"
"Yes."
"But what about works? Will I be saved if I have no works?"
"No."
"So I must have works to be saved?"
"Yes."
"But if I'm saved by faith alone, and works have nothing to do with my salvation, why do I need works?" And round and round I went.

It seemed that this argument was also carried on in Scripture: "For by grace are ye saved through faith; ... it is the gift of God: Not of works, lest any man should boast" (Eph. 2:8, 9, KJV). But on the other hand, "Was not Abraham our father justified by works" (James 2:21, KJV)? "Likewise also was not Rahab the harlot justified by works" (James 2:25, KJV)? "Ye see then how that by works a man is justified, and not by faith only" (James 2:24, KJV). And besides "the Son of man ... shall reward every man according to his works" (Matt. 16:27, KJV). No, that can't be right. We "are justified freely by his grace" (Rom. 3:24, NIV). "And if by grace, then it cannot be based on works; if it were, grace would no longer be grace." (Rom.11:6, NIV). Thus the argument raged on.

It wasn't until much later that I realized these apparent contradictions in Scripture weren't contradictions at all. I was simply stuck in the wrong paradigm, had the wrong idea of what works really were, and didn't understand the truth of Scripture.

Many Christians see works as bad. To them, works and legalism are synonymous. But Jesus admonished us to have works, "Let your light so shine before men," He said, "that they may see your good works, and glorify your Father which is in heaven (Matt. 5:16, KJV). And the apostle Paul said, "Be careful to maintain good works" (Titus 3:8, KJV). Notice these are not just any kind of works. These are *good* works.

What are *good* works? Christ was constantly doing good works. When He healed the man born blind, He referred to this as "works of God" (John 9:3, 4). And He told the Pharisees, "Many good works have I shewed you from my Father" (John 10:32, KJV). He was the epitome of good works and He said, "He that believeth on me, the works that I do shall he do also" (John 14:12, KJV).

An example of good works by a believer is found in Acts 9:36. "Now there was at Joppa a certain disciple named Tabitha, which by interpretation is called Dorcas: this woman was full of good works and almsdeeds which she did" (KJV). The NIV translation puts it this way: "In Joppa there was a disciple named Tabitha ... she was always *doing good and helping the poor"* (emphasis mine). And the apostle Paul, in describing what a faithful widow would be, defined good works as "bringing up children, showing hospitality, washing the feet of the Lord's people, helping those in trouble and devoting herself to all kinds of good deeds" (1 Tim. 5:10, NIV).

Good works are simply what the genuine Christian does. Not to get into God's good graces. That would be legalism. They simply do good deeds because they have allowed God to work in them "to will and to do of his good pleasure" (Phil. 2:13, KJV). When Scripture says our works justify us, it just means that good works validate the status of a right relationship with God. Like Abraham.

Now, no matter what the profession, if good works are not present, or are not genuine because they come from wrong motives, the person is not a true follower of Christ. Jesus made this clear when He said, "Not every one that saith unto me, Lord, Lord, shall enter into the kingdom of heaven; but he that doeth the will of my Father which is in heaven. Many will say to me in that day, 'Lord, Lord, have we not prophesied in thy name? and in thy name have cast out devils? and in thy name done many wonderful works?' And then will I profess unto them, I never knew you: depart from me, ye that work iniquity" (Matt. 7:21–23, KJV). Whatever "wonderful works" they did, they apparently came from wrong motives, were not the right stuff, and/or they were done through the power of the devil. These people were not in right relation to God. It was all a sham, a mere profession.

Christ said, "When the Son of Man comes in his glory, and all the angels with him, he will sit on his glorious throne. All the nations will be gathered before him, and he will separate the people one from another as a shepherd separates the sheep from the goats. He will put the sheep on his right and the goats on his left. Then the King will say to those on his right, 'Come, you who are blessed by my Father; take your inheritance, the kingdom prepared for you since the creation of the world. For I was hungry and you gave me something to eat, I was thirsty and you gave me something to drink, I was a stranger and you invited me in, I needed clothes and you clothed me, I was sick and you looked after me, I was in prison and you came to visit me.' Then the righteous will answer him, 'Lord, when did we see you hungry and feed you, or thirsty and give you something to drink? When did we see you a stranger and invite you in, or needing clothes and clothe you? When did we see you sick or in prison and go to visit you?' The King will reply, 'Truly I tell you, whatever you did for one of the least of these brothers and sisters of mine, you did for me'" (Matt. 25:31–40, NIV). These people exhibited the right stuff. Because of their relationship with God they just naturally performed deeds of love and mercy and were admitted into God's kingdom.

Continuing on with the passage, Jesus tells what happens to those who are not in right relation to God and therefore do not engage in good works, "Then he will say to those on his left, 'Depart from me, you who are cursed, into the eternal fire prepared for the devil and his angels. For I was hungry and you gave me nothing to eat, I was thirsty and you gave me nothing to drink, I was a stranger and you did not invite me in, I needed clothes and you did not clothe me, I was sick and in prison and you did not look after me'" (Matt. 25:41–43, NIV).

Good works are simply love expressed in action. They are deeds of love, mercy, and compassion. And from the true follower of Christ, they spring forth spontaneously.

Chapter 16
INTERCESSION

When I reflect on that fateful day in court when my friend and I were tried for our "crimes," I like to think the outcome would have been different had we had an attorney to intercede for us. I can see it now: Like Johnny Cochran did for O. J. Simpson, our attorney would have presented skillfully crafted arguments and gotten us off the hook. Or, if we were found guilty, he would have at least convinced the judge to pardon us. But no one interceded on our behalf, and we paid the penalty for our crimes.

The attorney-client scenario is analogous to a commonly held view of Christ's intercession for us in the heavenly court: God the Father is the Judge, Satan the prosecuting attorney, and Christ is our Advocate—our Attorney. And as our Attorney, He intercedes for us. He presents mighty arguments on our behalf, convinces the Judge to pardon us, and we are released from the punishment that is rightfully ours.

While it is true that Christ "ever liveth to make intercession" for us (Heb. 7:25), something is seriously wrong with this picture. It implies that God the Father doesn't love us as God the Son does, and He must be *persuaded* to forgive us. In an effort to get around this connotation some explain that the Father is not the problem. "It's the law," they say. "It's a legal problem, and the law demands the transgressor be punished. God is just, so He *must* mete out justice." But since the law is not a set of imposed rules, we are not in legal trouble with God or His law. So why do we need a defense attorney? Do we really need someone to intercede on our behalf?

A Frame of Reference

To understand the truth on this subject we must realize what Satan is up to. The devil is the one that's out to get us, not God. "Woe to the earth," John states, "because the devil has gone down to you! He is filled with fury, because he knows that his time is short" (Rev. 12:12, NIV). He "prowls around like a roaring lion looking for someone to devour" (1 Peter 5:8, NIV). And we are powerless against him, "For we wrestle not against flesh and blood, but against principalities, against powers, against the rulers of the darkness of this world, against spiritual wickedness in high places" (Eph. 6:12, KJV).

Satan's Strategies

Secondly, it is important to understand the devil's objective and the strategies he employs. His objective is to gain dominion over us, and the strategy he employs is deception, inducements, and force. He first presents himself as the one who can give us the desires of our heart and make us happy. He uses every method he can to make us believe this lie so we'll switch our allegiance. If that doesn't work, he tries a different approach. Through his agents (some of whom are scholars and members of the clergy), he paints God in a bad light. He portrays Him as being arbitrary, exacting, and full of vengeance if you get on His wrong side. Then Satan tries to overwhelm us with a sense of our rottenness and convince us that God would never accept someone as bad as we are. His goal is to discourage us to the point where we will finally give up and come fully under his control. Lastly, if all else proves unsuccessful, he aims to destroy. Because we have an enemy who is out to get us any way he can, we need Someone to intercede on our behalf. But what does this mean?

Illustrations of Intercession From Scripture

Zechariah's description of the interaction between the Lord and Satan concerning Joshua the high priest is a striking picture of intercession for sinners. Satan is standing beside the Lord, resisting His work and arguing that because Joshua is a sinner he rightfully belongs to him. He claims him as his subject and demands that Christ hand him over. But Christ, our Intercessor, responds to Satan's claims and says: "'The Lord rebuke you, Satan! The Lord, who has chosen Jerusalem, rebuke you! Is not this man a burning stick snatched from the fire?' Now Joshua was dressed in filthy clothes as he stood before the angel. The angel said to those who were standing before him, 'Take off his filthy clothes.' Then he said to Joshua, 'See, I have taken away your sin, and I will put fine garments on you.' Then I said, 'Put a clean turban on his head.' So they put a clean turban on his head and clothed him, while the angel of the LORD stood by" (Zech. 3:2-5, NIV).

Notice that it is not Christ working on the Father to accept us, pardon us, or to withhold punishment. Christ is represented here as doing battle with *Satan* on our behalf. He is interceding for us because we are helpless against Satan. It's a picture designed to give the worst sinner hope and assurance. Assurance that however bad we might be, God is for us and we shouldn't listen to the devil.

There's another way Christ intercedes for us. It's much like the intervention used on alcoholics. Because of their self-destructive thinking and behavior, they often need someone to help them see the truth of their situation. They need someone to help them realize what they are doing to themselves and others so they will admit their need and seek help. Without this insight, admission, and seeking, there is no hope for recovery. As sinners, we, too, need intervention. We have inherited an "alcoholic" nature and we need to be made to see our condition, and acknowledge our need before God can help us (1 John 1:8-10). And even after we agree with God's diagnosis and seek help, we still need Divine intervention on an ongoing basis because the devil is stalking us relentlessly. And when he tricks us into going his way and we engage in destructive thoughts and behavior, we need Someone to intercede on our behalf.

Consider the case of Peter at Christ's trial. When Peter denied he knew Christ, he needed intercession. He needed Someone to intervene and help him see what he was doing and get him back on track. And Christ came to the rescue. After the rooster crowed the third time, "The Lord turned and looked straight at Peter. Then Peter remembered the word the Lord had spoken to him" (Luke 22:61, NIV). Christ's look was not a look of anger, censure or resentment, but a look of love, pity, and compassion. And it melted Peter's heart. Scripture says, "he went outside and wept bitterly" (Luke 22:62, NIV). Christ knew ahead of time what Peter would do and He told him, "Simon, Simon, behold, Satan hath desired to have you, that he may sift you as wheat. But I have prayed for thee, that thy faith fail not: and when thou art converted, strengthen thy brethren" (Luke 22:31–32, KJV). What Christ told Peter before the denial, together with that look of unconditional love, was intercession, and it converted Peter.

All Members of the Godhead Intercede for Us

Christ is not the only one that intercedes for us. "In the same way, the Spirit helps us in our weakness. We do not know what we ought to pray for, but the Spirit himself intercedes for us with groans that words cannot express" (Rom. 8:26, NIV). Again, no one is begging the Father to be nice to us. The Spirit is *helping* us because we do not know what we ought to pray for. In essence God is saying, "don't worry about your prayers not being good enough for Me. The Spirit knows the deepest desires and longings of your heart and He will make sure the message gets through." It's another statement of assurance. Assurance that God hears and understands our prayers.

The good news is that God the Father, God the Son, and God the Holy Spirit, all intercede for us. The Father is directing the effort on our behalf. He sends angels that excel in strength to defend and protect us from Satan and his henchmen, and calms our fears through numerous assurances of His love. The Son came to this planet to personally intervene on our behalf. Not to protect us *from* the Father, but to lead us home *to* the Father. Just before he went back to heaven He told His disciples, "I say *not* unto you, that I will pray the Father for you: For *the Father himself loveth you*" (John 16:26, 27, KJV, emphasis mine). And the Holy Spirit joins in, enlightening, convicting, converting, and assuring.

Each member of the Trinity is saying and doing whatever is necessary to woo, protect and encourage us, and to give us the absolute assurance of God's unwavering, unconditional love. "What then are we to say about these things? If God is for us, who is against us? He who did not withhold his own Son, but gave him up for all of us, will he not with him also give us everything else? Who will bring any charge against God's elect? It is God who *justifies*. Who is to condemn? It is Christ Jesus ... *who indeed intercedes for us*. Who will separate us from the love of Christ? Will hardship, or distress, or persecution or famine, or nakedness, or peril, or sword?" "No, in all these things we are more than conquerors through him who loved us. For I am convinced that neither death nor life, neither angels nor demons, neither the present nor the future, nor any powers, neither height nor depth, nor anything else in all creation, will be able to separate us from the love of God that is in Christ Jesus our Lord" (Rom. 8:31–35, 37–39, NRSV, emphasis mine). *Intercession is God intervening in our behalf.*

Chapter 17
LEGALISM

It is not uncommon for Christians to define legalism as "trying to get to heaven by keeping the law." And since legalism does have to do with law, many believe that doing or not doing something stipulated in the Ten Commandments is automatically legalism. If I refrain from killing my obnoxious neighbor, or don't commit adultery with his wife, does that make me a legalist? Hardly. So what is it that constitutes legalism?

Legalism can take on many different forms. But common to all is the underlying conscious or unconscious belief that in order to be right with God we must bring or offer something to Him. Something that will cause Him to look on us with favor. Essentially this is a denial of our sin sick-condition and assumes the law to be an imposed set of rules. It shifts the focus from *our* condition and *our* need to what we perceive to be God's attitude and *His* need. Let me explain.

Legalism Has to Do With Trying to Get Into God's Good Graces

The Jews practiced what I call "classical legalism" and it goes something like this: God has imposed the rules, so keeping them must make Him happy. And if He is happy with me, He won't punish me and will take me to heaven. This legalist strives to be good by not being bad, bringing good behavior to God in an effort to win His favor.

Another form of legalism is also based on the belief that the law consists of imposed rules. But this form differs in that the belief is that the rules are impossible for humans to keep. Therefore, this legalist needs a Stand-in, a Substitute, to keep the rules for him. And since this legalist doesn't keep the rules he also needs a Stand-in to take the punishment he deserves for his disobedience. So, since Christ did both, he can bring this to God. This serves to satisfy God's "justice" and cause Him to look on him with favor. This form of legalism seems right, though, because now the person is "relying on Christ." He is bringing *Christ's* behavior to God as his obedience, and Christ's death as a penalty in payment for his disobedience. Given the assumption of an imposed law, either scenario is logical because from this frame of reference sin and salvation *are* legal, rule-keeping issues. And since we've all broken the rules, bringing good behavior to God to please Him—whether Christ's or mine—seems to makes sense. But no matter whose behavior we bring, at the bottom of it all lies the belief that to get right with God we must present something to effect a change in *Him* and, therefore, our standing with Him.

Legalism, Satan's Counterfeit Plan of Salvation

There's another even more subtle form of legalism. It goes back almost to the beginning of time. When Adam and Eve joined the rebellion, came under Satan's power and became infected with sin, God was ready with a plan of recovery. To help them understand the plan, the issues involved, and who would be responsible for what, He gave them a visual aid in the form of a ceremonial killing of a lamb. The ritual was designed to: 1) teach them that the natural consequence of living apart from God was this awful thing called death; 2) remind them, and be an acknowledgment of their condition and their need; 3) be a demonstration of their trust and dependence on God for their rescue and recovery; and 4) remind them of the Promised Savior to come. It was designed to benefit them, not from merely going through the motions, but from understanding and agreeing with what it all meant.

Satan, ever looking for an opportunity to distort the truth about God and thwart His plans, soon twisted its meaning into one of appeasement. He put forth the idea that God was angry with humans for breaking the rules, and that by bringing a sacrificial offering they were "making amends" for their disobedience. Of course they still had to keep the rules, but if they made mistakes the sacrifices would take care of those infractions, too. The Israelites bought into this idea, tried hard to obey the rules externally, *and* offered animal sacrifices in an effort to stay on the good side of God.

This is essentially how the pagans related to their god Molech. The only difference between them and the Jews was that the pagans didn't have any rules to keep. They just needed to appease Molech's wrath. So they offered their babies to be burned alive in his red-hot arms. Both pagans and Jews offered something to their god in an effort to effect a change in their standing with him. The Jews brought their behavior and animal sacrifices, and the pagans brought their babies. Neither did this in acknowledgment of *their* condition, *their* need, and *their* dependency. They did it because of the perceived need, character, and attitude of their god. Unfortunately, things haven't changed much. Human beings are still bringing all sorts of things to God, seeking to get into His good graces.

So, "With what *shall* I come before the Lord and bow down before the exalted God? Shall I come before him with burnt offerings, with calves a year old? Will the Lord be pleased with thousands of rams, with ten thousand rivers of olive oil? Shall I offer my firstborn for my transgression, the fruit of my body for the sin of my soul" (Mic. 6:6, 7, NIV, emphasis mine)?

If Micah had lived after the cross, he might well have added one more item to his list that constitutes legalism. That is, "Shall I come before Him with the blood of His Son?" The blood of God's Son? Yes. Does God require the blood of His Son to bring us into favor with Him? (Now, before you think I've done away with the atonement, please hear me out, and also read the next chapter). Let's let Micah answer: "He has showed you, O mortal, what is good. And what does the Lord require of you? To act justly and to love mercy and to walk humbly with your God" (Mic. 6:8, NIV). I submit to you that if we are relying on the blood of Jesus to change God's attitude toward us, we are practicing a very subtle form of legalism.

Does God's attitude toward us need changing? No! "*God* so loved the world that He gave His one and only Son" (John 3:16, NIV, emphasis mine). "God demonstrates *His own love* toward us, in that while we were yet sinners, Christ died for us" (Rom. 5:8, NASB, emphasis mine). And what was the message of the angels to the shepherds at Christ's birth? "Glory to God in the highest, and on earth peace, *good will toward men*" (Luke 2:14, KJV, emphasis mine). And Scripture says, "The Son radiates God's own glory and expresses the very character of God, and he sustains everything by the mighty power of his command" (Heb. 1:3, NLT). Did Jesus' attitude toward sinners need to be changed? No! Did anyone have to *earn* His favor? No! Jesus healed and forgave sinners whether they asked or not. He even exhibited an attitude of love and forgiveness toward those who were killing Him.

The Principle of Legalism

The essence of *legalism is the attitude of relying on or trusting in anything to effect a change in God and therefore our standing with Him.* What we do, or refrain from doing does not necessarily constitute legalism. It is *why* we do or don't do something. The *motive* determines whether our behavior or attitude is legalism or not. Legalism is the devil's counterfeit to the plan of salvation. And practicing it, knowingly or unknowingly, is a dead-end street. Why? Because, by thinking God or His Law must be reconciled to us, we ignore the fact that we are the ones in bondage and are sick and in need of deliverance and healing. Thus we make it impossible for God to save us because "we flatly deny God's diagnosis of our condition and cut ourselves off from what he has to say to us" (1 John 1:10, Phillips).

Chapter 18
ATONEMENT

If there's one thing a husband should never do, it's to forget his wife's birthday or their anniversary. It is an almost unpardonable offense that requires some act of "atonement." So, in an effort to obtain forgiveness and bring about reconciliation, the errant husband may bring her a gift box of chocolates or a bouquet of roses. In this way he hopes to get back into her good graces. Is this the way atonement works between God and us? Must some act be performed or gift offered to obtain God's forgiveness and get back into His good graces?

Two Views of Atonement

The most prominent views of the atonement within mainstream Christianity are founded on one of two basic assumptions. Each starts from a different premise and therefore each comes to a different conclusion. One view, akin to the example above, starts from the premise that God must be reconciled to man. The other is just the opposite. Its premise is that man must be reconciled to God. Though there are variations on the following explanations, all are based on one or the other or a curious mix of these two views.

The first view of atonement—that God must be reconciled to man—has its roots in paganism and was carried over and adapted to Christianity. It holds the unspoken assumption that the law is imposed rules; views sin as breaking the rules; believes we are in legal trouble with God because of our disobedience, and embraces the notion that suffering is an offset for our sin.

This is not just my idea. Christian theologian Van A. Harvey, in his book *A Handbook of Theological Terms,* explains this predominate view within Christianity. He says, "The disobedience of man is regarded as nothing less than an affront to the infinite majesty and honor of God. Such an affront requires infinite SATISFACTION. But since no creature can offer such a satisfaction, God himself must offer it, although in the form of man, since it is in behalf of man. God becomes man in order to satisfy his own offended honor" (p. 34). Harvey says this view "has been determinative so far as R.C. [Roman Catholicism] and Prot [Protestant] ORTHODOXY are concerned, although in the latter tradition a penal element is added and stressed; i.e., Christ is believed to have taken upon himself the punishment properly due man and thus satisfied God's just demands."

Now some theologians and Christian scholars have reasoned that because Christ *Himself* has taken on "the punishment properly due man and thus satisfied God's just demands" this is not paganistic. But the basic premise remains the same in that God must be reconciled to man and suffering is an offset for sin. Mr. Harvey has labeled this view as "ORTHODOXY," which means the quality or state of being orthodox, and orthodox means conforming to established doctrine.

Unfortunately, this "established doctrine" maligns God's character of love and causes many thoughtful people to reject true Christianity. And no wonder. One man who did just that reasoned, "The visiting on Adam's descendants through hundreds of generations dreadful penalties for a small transgression which they did not commit; the damning of all men who do not avail themselves of an alleged mode of obtaining forgiveness, which most men have never heard of; and the effecting a reconciliation by sacrificing a son who was perfectly innocent, to satisfy the assumed propitiatory victim; are modes of action which, ascribed to a human ruler, would call forth expressions of abhorrence: and the ascription of them to the Ultimate Cause of things, even now felt to be full of difficulties, must be impossible" (George MacDonald, *Knowing The Heart of God*, Bethany House Publishers, pp. 17, 18).

Permit me to examine this belief a bit further. If the law consisted of imposed rules, as this view assumes, God could choose to *not* impose a penalty on those who break the rules, couldn't He? Since He is all forgiving and all merciful, He could just forgive without *anyone* "paying," couldn't He? If He wanted to? "Well, no," some say, "God is *so* holy and *so* just that His justice had to be satisfied and the sinner punished." But why would God *have to* punish someone? In this view it's because our disobedience—breaking the rules—offends Him. He has been dishonored and His wrath can be only be assuaged and His honor restored if someone pays.

In an honest effort to get around this picture of God some say, "No, He's not the problem, it's the law. The law must be satisfied." But if God *imposed* the rules as this theology implies, He could change or repeal the rules anytime He wanted to, couldn't He? Or is it like the law of the Medes and the Persians? Once a king made a rule, even he couldn't change it! But that doesn't make sense either because if God in His sovereignty imposed the rules, why would they bind *Him*? Is the law a higher authority than God Himself? If He made the rules and imposed them, then who is it that needs to be satisfied, the law or the Law Maker? And why would He impose rules on us when in His foreknowledge He would have known that everyone would break them anyway? What's the point?

Any way you look at this so-called Christian theology it makes God look bad. In fact, it makes Him look like a tyrant. We recoil from the practice of the heathens in the Old Testament who sacrificed their babies to appease their god Molech. But it seems many Christians have applied this same notion to our Creator God—that He too must be reconciled to us. That someone must pay to turn aside His wrath.

Originally atonement was pronounced "at-one-ment," meaning the parties were "at one" with each other. But somewhere along the line "at one" became "atone" and "at-one-ment" became "atonement." And not only did the pronunciation change but so did the meaning.

From meaning a *state* of unity and agreement, this word came to mean an *act* performed to assuage wrath. And as we have seen, many theologians and laity alike now view "atonement" as "assuaging the wrath" of God; an act that pays for wrongdoing; an act that causes or allows God to forgive.

Unfortunately this view has now found its way into dictionaries, hymns, and some translations and paraphrases of Scripture. For example, Romans 3:25 in The New Living Translation reads, "For God sent Jesus to take the punishment for our sins and to satisfy God's anger against us." And in the 3rd edition of the New World Dictionary of American English the word "atonement" is defined as *"assuaging the wrath*; reconciliation, agreement (obsolete); theologically, the redeeming of mankind and the *reconciliation of God with man* brought about by Jesus' sufferings and death" (emphasis mine). Because God is represented this way it's not surprising that many don't want anything to do with Him.

The Second View of "Atonement"

The second view of atonement–that man needs to be reconciled to God–sees the law as natural, descriptive, fixed. It recognizes that man turned away from God; that man needs to be brought back to the relationship, and acknowledges that man is "sick" and in need of healing. Looking back at the dictionary definition of atonement, you will see the words, "agreement (obsolete)." From this we can see that at one time the meaning of this word described the *state* of a relationship. This is also borne out in the way it was spelled and pronounced–at-one-ment. It meant that the parties were "at one" with each other, the opposite of estrangement. It meant the relationship was close and harmonious.

In this view God doesn't need to be persuaded to forgive us and have a relationship with us, He *already wants one.* We're the ones that need persuading. Listen to God the Son as He prays to the Father for us,

"I want all of them to be one with each other, just as I am one with you and you are one with me. *I also want them to be one with us.* Then the people of this world will believe that you sent me" (John 17:21, CEV, emphasis mine). Listen to Him as He grieves over those who refuse to come to Him: "O Jerusalem, Jerusalem! You that murder the prophets and stone those who have been sent to you! How often I have desired to gather your children to me, as a hen gathers her chickens under her wings, and you would not come!" (Matt. 23:37, NTMS). Clearly God is pursuing *us*! And the apostle Paul proclaims this truth when he says, "God was reconciling *the world to himself ... not counting people's sins against them*" (2 Cor. 5:19, NIV, emphasis mine).

The truth of this view is also borne out by looking at what went wrong between God and Adam and Eve. In the beginning there was at-one-ment—perfect peace, harmony, and open communication between God and man. They were at one with each other. But as Adam and Eve began to listen Satan's lies, they began to distrust God, and as a result, their oneness with Him was broken. They left God for another, and became estranged.

When God came to talk to them about the problem, they were afraid, and hid in the bushes (Gen. 3:8–10). Why were they afraid? The implication is that they thought God was angry with them. Was He? No. Was He offended? No. He was sad. Very sad. Did *He* sever the relationship? No. The problem was with Adam and Eve. *They* believed the devil's lies about God and became estranged. *They* became "alienated from God and were enemies in [*their*] minds" (Col. 1:21, NIV, emphasis mine).

To salvage the situation and restore the relationship, the God who "so loved the world, gave his one and only Son" (John 3:16, NIV) to come to this planet "to reconcile to himself all things" (Col. 1:20, NIV). Not to make peace by appeasing an angry, offended Father God. Not to pay a blood penalty demanded by His Father to "satisfy His just demands" so He would forgive. No! "God is for us" (Rom. 8:31, NIV). Christ came to make the character of the Father known, to set the record straight about Him. He came to rescue man from an enemy who had deceived him and turned him against God. He came to win man back into at-one-ment with the Father.

But Isn't the Cross the Atonement?

Now if Christ's death on the cross wasn't to provide "infinite satisfaction" to an offended God, if it wasn't to reconcile Him to us, and cause or allow Him to forgive, what is the meaning of the cross? Are we doing away with its importance? Are we doing away with "the atonement"? God forbid! As Paul said, "May I never boast except in the cross of our Lord Jesus Christ" (Gal. 6:14, NIV). Without the cross we would have no hope. We could have no oneness with God. Yes, the cross is about "the shedding of blood" and according to Col. 1:20, we are reconciled to God "through his blood, shed on the cross." And so we sing, "There's Power in the Blood," "Redeemed by the Blood of the Lamb," and "There is a Fountain Filled with Blood." From all of this one could get the idea that there's some kind of strange magic or power in the blood. But the blood itself isn't what saves us. God does. If we rely on the blood to make us right with God it would be a form of idolatry—hematolatry, if you please. It would be paganistic.

Then what is it about the blood that reconciles us to God? It's what the blood stands for. The blood is simply a symbol of a deeper truth, the truth about God. And that is, that no matter how His creatures treat Him, His love is unstoppable. And His shed blood on the cross proves the lengths to which He will go to prove it.

Jesus Himself told us the purpose of the cross. He said, "And I, if I be lifted up from the earth, *will draw all [men] unto me*" (John 12:32, KJV, emphasis mine). (The word "men" is not in the in the original Greek, and therefore the KJV puts it in brackets.) The cross is meant to draw us back to God. And it has tremendous drawing power. Why? Because the cross is the crowning evidence of God's incredible, unconditional, unquenchable, unstoppable love. "When they hurled their insults at him, he did not retaliate; when he suffered, he made no threats" (1 Peter 2:23, NIV). As He was being hung on the cross, He forgave His killers, and they hadn't even asked. "Father, forgive them," He said, "for they do not know what they are doing" (Luke 23:34, NIV). The cross is our assurance of a love stronger than death. For anyone who is willing to take a serious look, the cross woos and wins him or her back to love and trust, back to at-one-ment with God.

Angels Needed the "Atonement" Too

It is evident from Scripture that the angels in heaven also needed at-one-ment. Because of Satan's lies they, too, must have had questions about God's character, for the apostle Paul said of Christ, "God was pleased to have all his fullness dwell in him, and through him to reconcile to himself all things, whether things on earth or *things in heaven*, by making peace through his blood, shed on the cross" (Col. 1:19, 20, NIV, emphasis mine). So because of what was revealed at the cross, the angels are brought back into full at-one-ment with God, confirmed in their loyalty to Him and forever guarded from rebellion. Christ predicted this in the verse previously quoted and is even clearer in the E. V. Rieu's translation: "And I, if I am lifted up from the earth, will draw *the whole creation* to myself" (John 12:32, emphasis mine).

The Cross Revealed Even More

Christ went to the cross to bring the whole universe into at-one-ment. And to everyone's comfort He showed what He does to those who don't accept His offer of healing. He exposed the fact that Satan was lying when he told Eve: "You will not certainly die" (Gen. 3:4, NIV). Implied in this statement is "God has lied to you. Don't trust Him. He is self-serving and doesn't want you knowing what He knows. He just wants to keep you in subjection to Him. Believe me, *nothing* will happen to you." God had to expose Satan's statement as the lie that it was. And He couldn't do it any other way but to show what actually happens to those who reject Him. So "God made him who had no sin to be sin for us" (2 Cor. 5:21, NIV). And He died the sinner's death. What is the "sinner's death?" *How* will they die? Will God kill them? Will He burn them in hell? And what about God's wrath? The cross provides the answers. What did God do to His Son? Did He kill Him? Did He burn Jesus in hell? Did Jesus suffer the wrath of God? No, no, and yes. This is another area where the devil has been enormously successful in maligning the character of God. He has succeeded in getting us to put the sinful attribute of human anger on God. God's anger is not like human anger. The apostle Paul explains it in Romans 1. "The wrath of God is being revealed from heaven against all the godlessness and wickedness of men who suppress the truth by their wickedness."

He goes on to describe the nature of this wickedness and then explains what God's wrath actually is—what He did to these wicked people: "Therefore *God gave them over* in the sinful desires of their hearts to sexual impurity for the degrading of their bodies with one another." Paul then describes more wickedness and again explains what God does: "Because of this, God *gave them over* to shameful lusts." Again Paul describes the wickedness of people, and again explains God's wrath: "Furthermore, just as they did not think it worthwhile to retain the knowledge of God, so *God gave them over* to a depraved mind, so that they do what ought not to be done" (Rom 1:18, 24, 26, 28, NIV, emphasis mine).

In the original language, Paul used the same terminology to explain what the Father did to Christ on the cross. He "*gave him up* for us all" (Rom. 8:32, NIV, emphasis mine). He didn't do anything *to* Him. But you say, "he endured the suffering that should have been ours, the pain that we should have borne" (Isa. 53:4, GNB). That's true, but let's finish the verse: "All the while *we thought* that his suffering *was punishment* sent by God." emphasis mine. But it *wasn't*. We just *thought* it was.

As Jesus hung on the cross He felt the oneness with His Father breaking up. He couldn't stand it, and "Jesus cried out in a loud voice, *'Eli, Eli, lema sabachthani?'* (which means, 'My God, my God, *why have you forsaken me?*')" (Matt. 27:46, NIV, emphasis mine)? God was giving Him up. And Jesus died of a broken heart. He experienced what happens to those who reject God and it killed Him.

If we finally reach the point where there is nothing more that God can do to win us back to love and trust, He will finally leave us to the choice we have made. We will suffer the natural consequences of trying to live apart from Him who is love. Isaiah calls it God's "strange act" (Isa. 28:21). God treats them as He said about Ephraim in Hosea 4:17: "Ephraim is joined to idols; leave him alone!" (NIV). If we insist on going our own way, what more can God do?

God wants all His creatures to see the issues involved in this great conflict between good and evil. He wants us to be able make an intelligent decision about the leaders from which we have to choose, and to understand the consequences of the two options we have. All must know the truth about God's character including what He does to those who refuse at-one-ment. The devil's lies must be shown for what they are, for "God must prove true, though every man be false; as the scripture says, 'That you may be shown to be upright in what you say, and win your case when you go into court'" (Rom. 3:4, Goodspeed). God's way is the way of love and truth—backed by evidence. And Christ's life and death provides it all.

What "Atonement" Is

Atonement is the state of being fully reconciled to God. Not just a mental assent, but an in-the-heart-reconcilement to Him. It means the absence of any barriers between God and us. It is an embracing and acceptance of His love for us. It is to be restored to a loving, trusting, saving relationship with our Creator God. The term "*the* atonement" is kind of a misnomer. But if we must use the term, it means *all* that God has done and is still doing to bring His children back to a loving, trusting relationship with Him. On earth it was not just what happened on the cross, but *all* Christ's work. It is what He taught, the way He lived, and the way He died. Jesus said, "I am the way and the truth and the life. No one comes to the Father except through me" (John 14:6–7, NIV). That is, Jesus is the only way to come to the Father because it is only through Him that we can really know the Father. So "*Christ died* for sins once for all ... *in order to lead you to God*" (1 Peter 3:18, GNB, emphasis mine).

Do you believe the message of the cross? "Or do you show contempt for the riches of his kindness, forbearance and patience, not realizing that God's kindness is intended to lead you toward repentance" (Rom 2:4, NIV)? I know, "the message of the cross is foolishness to those who are perishing, but to us who are being saved it is the power of God" (1 Cor. 1:18, NIV). For "This is how God showed his love among us: He sent his one and only Son into the world that we might live through him" (1 John 4:9, NIV). And if we believe, and come to Him, trusting in His goodness, the relationship is re-established and there is at-one-ment. *Atonement means at-one-ment, and at-one-ment means to be at one with God.* It means to be in union with Him.

Chapter 19
SANCTIFICATION

Sanctification isn't talked about much these days. Maybe it's because of what it means in the life of the Christian. It gets too personal. Too internal. But because "this is the will of God, even your sanctification" (1 Thess. 4:3, KJV), a Christian cannot safely ignore or reject that for which this word stands.

In Scripture, the English word "sanctification" is always translated from the Greek word, *hagiasmos*. And "sanctify" is translated from the word *hagiazo*, which means to make holy, or to purify. In checking Webster's New Collegiate Dictionary I was surprised to find that "sanctify" means "to free from sin: purify." So I think we're safe in saying that "sanctification" means the action or process of being freed or purified from sin.

In chapter 2 we concluded that 1 John 3:4 really is true, that sin really is transgression of the law. And now we see that sanctification is the process of being freed or purified from sin. Therefore to *be* sanctified means to be in harmony with the law. Furthermore, since the law is all about love, and God's very nature is love, sanctification must be the process of being conformed to the likeness of God's character of love. In other words, it is becoming like God in our thoughts, desires and actions—becoming loving in nature. "For this is the Message you have heard from the beginning—that we are to love one another" (1 John 3:11, WNT). By what means does this take place? Judicial act? Vicarious substitution? By disciplined effort? Does it happen in the record books in heaven or in a literal sense? Do we accomplish it, does God accomplish it, or is it a joint effort?

The good news is that God's "divine power has given us everything we need for life and godliness through our knowledge of Him who called us by his own glory and goodness." This means that we "may participate in the divine nature, having escaped the corruption in the world caused by evil desires" (2 Peter 1:3, 4, NIV). Notice that this happens in a literal sense—we can *"participate* in the divine nature." How does it happen? According to the above text it happens *through our knowledge of Him.*

But this doesn't happen from *what* you know. It's *who* you know. It is accomplished through knowing God personally, intimately, and wanting His character to be ours. In the above passage The Living Bible quotes Peter this way: "Do you want more and more of God's kindness and peace? Then learn to know him better and better. For as you know him better and better, he will give you, through his great power, everything you need for living a truly good life: he even shares his own glory and his own goodness with us! And by that same mighty power he has given all the other rich and wonderful blessings he promised; for instance, the promise to save us from the lust and rottenness all around us, and to give us his own character" (2 Peter 1:2–4).

As you can see from the above passage we have a part to play in this process too. We have to actively seek to know Him better and better, really want His character to be ours, and act accordingly. Jesus Himself said, "Blessed are they which do hunger and thirst after righteousness: for they shall be filled" (Matt. 5:6, KJV). Or as the Good News Bible translates this verse, "Happy are those whose greatest desire is to do what God requires; God will satisfy them fully!" The apostle Paul explains that it is by focusing on Jesus, the Way, the Truth and the Life—by studying Him, the Word—His death *and His life,* by getting to know Him personally, that we become changed into His likeness. He said, "we all, with open face beholding as in a glass the glory of the Lord [His character], *are changed into the same image* [His image] from glory to glory, even as by the Spirit of the Lord" (2 Cor. 3:18, KJV, emphasis mine). It is a fixed law of the mind that we become like what we focus on. It works for us the same as it worked for Israel of old. "When they came to Mount Peor, they began to worship Baal and soon became as disgusting as the gods they loved" (Hos. 9:10, GNB). I believe we can have such a close relationship with God, that we will automatically do His will. For "if anyone obeys God's word, God's love is truly made complete in that person" (1 John 2:5, NIrV).

Sanctification is the action or process of becoming loving in nature. It's the process of having the mind of Christ implanted in us (Phil. 2:5). It is the fulfillment of the New Covenant promise: "'This is the agreement that I will make with them in those later days,' says the Lord, 'I will put my laws into their minds, and write them upon their hearts'" (Heb. 10:16, Goodspeed). And that's good news.

Chapter 20
THE GOSPEL

Glancing out the window during my early morning devotions, I was startled to see a huge, red and yellow hot air balloon heading toward our house. Floating majestically through the air in the stillness of the summer morning it was a beautiful sight to behold. Scrambling for our shoes and appropriate clothing, my wife and I ran outside just as it came lower to the ground.

"Grab the tether lines and hold on," called the pilot. We did as instructed and secured the craft so it wouldn't drift away until the chase car could arrive. The pilot was a friendly fellow and answered our many questions about his marvelous contraption. Imagine our surprise when he invited us to go up for a bird's-eye view of the landscape. What an opportunity! We marveled at the power of hot air to lift humans and craft into the heavens.

The gospel is like hot air. Silent, unseen, powerful. So powerful that when received into the heart it can lift us up from the pit of sin and seat us in "heavenly places" (Eph. 2:6). The apostle Paul called it "the power of God unto salvation" (Rom. 1:16). He also said, "If anyone preaches to you a gospel that is different from the one you have accepted, may he be condemned to hell" (Gal. 1:9, GNB). Pretty strong words! Why would he say that? Because, he knew that for it to be "the power of God unto salvation," it must be the real thing. Any other "gospel" would be a fake gospel. And like filling a balloon with cold air, it would have no power to lift us up.

The devil knows the gospel has power, so he sells a counterfeit. And he uses Christians to do it. Christians? Of course. Non-Christians don't preach the gospel. What's more, he even uses scholars and theologians. Now, I doubt any sincere preacher, theologian or Christian scholar *purposefully* preaches or teaches a counterfeit gospel. If they do, it must be because they don't know any better. But Paul did warn about "false apostles, deceitful workmen, masquerading as apostles of Christ." "Satan himself," he said, "masquerades as an angel of light. It is not surprising, then, if his servants masquerade as servants of righteousness" (2 Cor. 11:13-15, NIV). Though Paul was addressing a problem in his day, the sad truth is that some still promote a spurious gospel today.

Lots of "Good News"

The gospel, or good news, is generally thought of as "Christ died for my sins." And that's biblical (1 Cor. 15:1-3). But Christ Himself preached the gospel *before* His crucifixion and His message wasn't about the cross. (See Matt. 4:23; 9:35; Luke 4:18.) He also sent His disciples out to preach the gospel before He died and their message wasn't about His coming death and resurrection either. At that time they had no comprehension of what was going to happen to Him and what it would all mean. (See Luke 9:6; 10:1-9.) So there must be more to the gospel than just "Christ died for my sins." And there is.

There's lots of "good news" in Scripture. There's the good news of salvation (Eph. 1:13); the good news of Christ's death, burial, and resurrection (1 Cor. 15:1-4); The good news of the kingdom (Matt. 4:23; 24:14); the good news of peace (Eph. 6:15); the good news of healing, deliverance, and restoration (Luke 4:18); the good news of Christ (Mark 1:1), and the good news of God (Rom. 1:1). If we are to fulfill the great Gospel Commission from Christ to "Go into all the world and preach the good news to all creation" (Mark 16:15, NIV), what should we preach? Whatever we preach, if we don't preach the good news that Christ commissioned us to preach, would we be preaching a spurious gospel? Would we be one of those "deceitful workmen" the apostle Paul was talking about, preaching a "gospel" devoid of power?

The Good News About What?

The gospel that Jesus preached was about "the kingdom" (Matt. 4:23, KJV). And according to Him, it is this Good News that "will be preached through all the world for a witness to all people; and then the end will come" (Matt. 24:14, GNB). So, what is this kingdom Jesus referred to? And what is the news that's so good?

The promise of the coming Messiah was everything to the Jews because they knew that when He came He would set up *the* kingdom. To them this meant He would free them from the hated Romans, establish an earthly kingdom on the ruins of the other nations and elevate them to international supremacy. So, to them, when John the Baptist announced, "The kingdom of heaven is at hand," it was *very* good news. That meant the Messiah was here! But after three years, and still no sign of any kingdom, some Pharisees "asked Jesus when the Kingdom of God would come. His answer was, 'The Kingdom of God does not come in such a way as to be seen. No one will say, 'Look, here it is!' or, 'There it is!'; because *the Kingdom of God is within you* "(Luke 17:20, 21, GNB, emphasis mine). In other words, don't look around for some earthly power as evidence that the kingdom is here. God's kingdom is not visible. It's inside you. What did He mean by that?

The kingdoms or countries of this world reign over their citizens by force of imposed laws. These laws consist of rules that apply to external behavior, and threaten punishment for those who disobey. But there is another kind of kingdom that "reigns" over each one of us. It is an internal one. And that is, whatever principle or philosophy we adopt or embrace, whatever motivates us from within, whatever we live by, is what rules us. Christ did not come to set up a physical, earthly kingdom. He came to set up a spiritual kingdom by implanting a new principle in the hearts and minds of human beings. But this was not the kind of kingdom the Pharisees wanted. To them this was not good news.

The kingdom of heaven, or the kingdom of God, begins in the heart (mind), and is set up in us when we accept, embrace, and become subject to the law of this kingdom, the royal law of love (James 2:8). This is not an external subjection to the obedience of rules. It is the law of love reigning in our hearts. It is a fulfillment of the new covenant promise to write this law in our hearts so we will love naturally. This kingdom is referred to in Scripture in various ways: it is stated as being born again (John 3:5); Christ in us (Col. 1:27, John 17: 26); Christ formed in us (Gal. 4:19); the word of Christ in us (Col. 3:16, John 15:7); the Spirit in us (Rom. 8: 9, 1 Cor. 3:16, 2 Cor. 1:22); God living in us by His Spirit (Eph. 2:22); having our minds controlled by the Spirit (Rom. 8:6); eating His flesh and drinking His blood (John 6:53); being transformed by the renewing of the mind (Rom. 12:2); having Christ's mind in us (Phil.2:5); partaking of the Divine nature (2 Peter 1:3, 4); the purifying of our hearts by faith (Acts 15:9); the law written in our hearts (Rom. 2:15, Heb. 8:10); and having the love of God shed abroad in our hearts (Rom. 5:5).

Now for the News

Now, the news about this kingdom is only relevant, good, and powerful in the context and realization of the bad news, and the truth about what God is really like. The bad news is the situation and condition in which we find ourselves. Held hostage by the "god of this world," we are under his rule and subject to the law of his kingdom—"the law of sin and death" (Rom. 8:2). The good news is that which Isaiah prophesied the Messiah would say about Himself and His work when He came. "The spirit of the Lord God is upon me," he said, "because the Lord has anointed me; he has sent me to bring good news to the oppressed, to bind up the brokenhearted, to proclaim liberty to the captives, and release to the prisoners" (Isa. 61:1, NRSV). This is the very passage that Jesus read in the Nazareth synagogue. He then applied this to Himself by saying. "What you have just heard me read has come true today" (Luke 4:21, CEV). The good news is that God in the person of Jesus, the Messiah, came to our planet to liberate us from Satan's rule and the law of his kingdom, which is death. Christ came to give us life by establishing the law of His kingdom, which is the law of love, within us.

But God does not force Himself on us. Our allegiance to Him and His kingdom must be freely given. For us to voluntarily choose Him as king, He must be someone we would like and could trust. Knowing this, the god of this world developed a strategy of character assassination against the true King. He painted God as a king who is severe, unforgiving, arbitrary, capricious and vengeful. God could not answer these charges with claims. He must provide evidence to set the record straight. The truth about the King must be revealed. That's why "the Son of God has come and has given us understanding *so that we may know him* who is true ... He is the true God and eternal life" (1 John 5:20, NRSV, emphasis mine). To that end Jesus promised us, "ye shall know the truth, and the truth shall make you free" (John 8:32, KJV).

When His work on earth was almost completed Jesus told His Father, "I have made your self known to them and will continue to do so" For what purpose? Jesus answers: "*that the love which you have had for me may be in their hearts*–and that I may be there also" (John 17:26, Phillips, emphasis mine). We will only be liberated from Satan's rule and have the kingdom of heaven established in us if we know the truth about the character of the Father.

Now we can understand Paul's statement about how he felt about the gospel and why he said things like, "I am not ashamed of the Good News; it is the power of God which brings Salvation to everyone who believes in Christ ... For in it there is a revelation of the Divine Righteousness" (Rom. 1:16, TCNT). And things like, "if anyone preaches to you a gospel that is different from the one you have accepted, may he be condemned to hell" (Gal. 1:9, GNB).

Earlier, in our discussion of the word "righteousness," we saw that God's righteousness is His love. So Romans 1:16 can legitimately be paraphrased as, "I am not ashamed of the good news because it is God's powerful way of saving everyone who believes it. For in it God's redeeming love is revealed." So the good news reveals God's love. Is it powerful? Absolutely! It's the most powerful thing in the universe! But in order for it to be powerful in us it must first be believed and accepted. And in order for it to be believed and received it must be made known to us. That's why "in the past God spoke to our ancestors many times and in many ways through the prophets, but in these last days he has spoken to us through his Son.... He reflects the brightness of God's glory and is the exact likeness of God's own being" (Heb. 1:1–3, GNB).

So, the gospel, or good news, is that *"God loved the world so much that he gave his only Son, so that everyone who believes in him may not die but have eternal life"* (John 3:16, GNB, emphasis mine). God gave us His Son so that through Him we might be rescued from Satan's rule and become citizens of the heavenly kingdom, be subject to the law of life, and live forever. To believe in Him means to believe and trust Him as our Deliverer, to give Him our voluntary allegiance, to open our heart's door to Him, and allow Him to write the law of the kingdom on our hearts. If we do this, we can say with Paul, praise be to God, for "He has rescued us from the dominion of darkness and brought us into the kingdom of the Son he loves" (Col. 1:13, NIV).

Chapter 21
ALLEGIANCE

The awful events of September 11, 2001, with the resultant loss of life and destruction, electrified and unified America like nothing else in recent history. Not since the attack on Pearl Harbor have we seen the display of more patriotism. Tributes to America flooded the Internet. "God Bless America" and "United We Stand" slogans were seen everywhere. Flags were flown from flagpoles and vehicle antennas. They were pasted in windows and on vehicles of every kind imaginable. They appeared on lapels, draped on the sides of commercial and private buildings, and painted on walls. People wore t-shirts, hats and other clothing that proudly displayed our national emblem. Sales of flags soared, and in many cities supply could not keep up with the demand. Schools emphasized the recitation of "The Pledge of Allegiance." And on October 11, the one-month anniversary of the attack on America, people all across America stopped at a specified time to pledge their allegiance to the flag and the republic for which it stands. The events of that unforgettable day led to a renewed focus on what this country is all about and the freedom the flag represents.

Military personnel are especially passionate about the flag, particularly in times of war. Several years ago an article appeared in *The Reader's Digest* that vividly illustrates the deep meaning our flag embodies. In this inspiring story Leo Thorsness relates the experience of some U.S. servicemen who were taken prisoners of war in Vietnam. One day a young naval pilot named Mike found remnants of what was once a white handkerchief. Sneaking it into his cell, Mike began fashioning it into a flag. For days he scrubbed and cleaned the grimy rag. Then, using bits of ground up roof tiles for red and blue, he painted the colors onto the cloth. Using thread from his only blanket and a bamboo sliver for a needle, he sewed on stars.

Early one morning after he had finished, when the guards were not paying attention, Mike held up his masterpiece and whispered loudly from the back of the cell. "Hey gang, look here!"

Thorsness says when Mike raised the makeshift flag, "We automatically stood straight and saluted, our chests puffing out, and more than a few eyes had tears."

Later, during a shakedown, the guards found Mike's flag. That night they hauled him from his cell and beat him mercilessly. Around daylight, badly broken and his voice gone, they dumped him back in his cell. But Thorsness says that within two weeks Mike had scrounged another piece of cloth and began to make another flag! Why? In the face of the consequences he had just experienced, why would he risk his life by making another one? And why did his captors react so violently over a dirty old rag? Because, to those captive soldiers that rag-flag stood for something, and the Viet Cong knew it.

Christians, too, have a flag. It's not the one seen standing proudly by the American flag in many churches. It's not a physical symbol. It's a symbol in time. It's the Sabbath. As Christians, we know we have a terrorist who silently goes about his work to terrorize and destroy while holding us hostage on this planet. God foresaw all this and knew we would need a "national" emblem to rally around. He knew we would need something that would always be there to remind us of our heavenly country and the One to whom we belong. So, on the last day of creation God raised His "flag" by giving us the Sabbath. And like our U.S. flag, this flag, too, stands for freedom. To the Sabbathkeeping Christian it's a reminder of who we are, who our Father is, and that His love for us is unstoppable. Every week it becomes a reminder of what God has done, what He is doing, and what He will do to affect our rescue from the enemy and ensure our freedom forever.

I love my earthly country because of the values of freedom embodied in its constitution. And because I understand and agree with that for which it stands, I pledge my allegiance to its symbol, the flag. Likewise I love my heavenly country because of the values of freedom embodied in its constitution, the great Law of Love. What's more, I love my heavenly Father for the way He governs and what that says about Him. Therefore,

> I pledge allegiance to the Sabbath
> Of the Lord God of the universe
> And to the kingdom for which it stands
> One universe, under God, indivisible,
> With liberty and love for all.

Would those servicemen have saluted the Viet Cong flag? My guess is they would have died rather than pledge their allegiance to it.

To whom do you pledge your allegiance? Which "flag" will you salute? The enemy's or the Creator's? Choose you this day whom you will serve. As for me, I pledge my allegiance to the Sabbath of the Lord my God because I understand and embrace that for which it stands.

Chapter 22
PUTTING IT ALL TOGETHER

Whether we like it or not, we are all caught up in the war between good and evil: the war between Satan, the originator of evil and God, the origin of love. Using character assassination as a weapon, Satan's plan was to turn the angels against God and take over the government of the universe. Though he was successful in gaining the allegiance of one third of the angels, his attempted coup failed, and he, along with his followers were thrown out of heaven.

Rankled and bitter, he then bent his efforts to win over the inhabitants of planet earth and set up his government here. Using the same strategy of deceit, he lied about God and succeeded in getting our first parents to switch their allegiance. They rebelled against God's loving rule and became depraved. Their natures were changed and they became out of harmony with the unchangeable law of love–the law of life for the whole universe; and alienated from God, they would self-destruct. They passed on their depraved natures to their children, and Satan became the prince of this world.

Though Adam and Eve turned their backs on God, He did not abandon them. Through the revelation of His character of love He would draw them back to love and loyalty, back into harmony with the law of life. God said, "I will give them a heart to know me, that I am the Lord. They will be my people, and I will be their God, for they will return to me with all their heart" (Jer. 24:7, NIV).

The truth about us is we all have inherited this "disease" called sin. But if we admit our condition and our utter inability to change ourselves, if we realize our desperate need of God's healing power and are willing to listen and choose the way of love, He is more than eager to heal the damage that Satan has done to us and restore us to what he designed us to be. (See 1 John 1:8-10.) Listen to His promise: "I will put my laws in their minds and write them on their hearts. I will be their God, and they will be my people" (Heb. 8:10, NIV).

Most of the world is still alienated from God. They are still under the deceptive power of the Evil One. His strategy has been so successful that even many who call themselves Christian now hold a flawed belief system. They believe our problem is a legal one. They believe that the law is a set of imposed rules; that we have broken the rules and therefore God has something against us. And, in order for Him to forgive us some act must be performed to assuage His wrath. Our adversary has put forth the idea that God will forever torture in hell anyone who does not accept Him. Consequently, many have rejected God, and rightly so. Many others who haven't given up on God (lay people, scholars, and clergy alike) are now trapped in a false belief system; a belief system that has no power to save; a belief system that makes God look like a despot.

Common sense tells us that how we relate to someone comes from our opinion of that person. And if our belief system doesn't tell the truth about God, what He wants of us, and what He will do to those who do not accept what He has to offer, we won't be able have a personal, intimate, saving relationship with Him. The bottom line is that any belief system that doesn't make God look good, is not telling the truth.

The real truth about God is that He is better than anyone can describe. In fact, He is infinitely better than anyone can imagine Him to be! And whether or not we accept Him, His love for us is unconditional and unstoppable; and there is nothing we can do or not do that will cause Him to love us less, or persuade Him to love us more.

"In view of all this, what can we say? If God is for us, who can be against us? Certainly not God, who did not even keep back his own Son, but offered him for us all! He gave us his Son—will he not also freely give us all things? ... Who, then, can separate us from the love of Christ? ... For I am certain that nothing can separate us from his love: neither death nor life, neither angels nor other heavenly rulers or powers, neither the present nor the future, neither the world above nor the world below—there is nothing in all creation that will ever be able to separate us from the love of God which is ours through Christ Jesus our Lord" (Rom 8:31, 32, 38, 39, GNB).

"So then, just as you received Christ Jesus as Lord, continue to live your lives in him ... See to it that no one takes you captive through hollow and deceptive philosophy" (Col. 2:6–8, NIV). "And now all glory to him who alone is God, who saves us through Jesus Christ our Lord; ... he is able to keep you from slipping and falling away, and to bring you, sinless and perfect, into his glorious presence with mighty shouts of everlasting joy. Amen" (Jude 24, 25, LB).

Appendix
WHY GOD COMMANDED LOVE

When Jesus was asked which of the Commandments was the most important, He said there were two: to love God and to love our neighbor as ourselves (Matt. 22:36–40). In fact, He said, all the Commandments are based on these two principles. So when God gave the Ten Commandments, He was essentially commanding the Israelites to love. Now common sense tells us that no matter how hard we might try, we cannot make ourselves love a neighbor we don't like, even when commanded to do so. I found this to be all too true when we moved to into a new house. For some reason our neighbor seemed determined to vex and harass my family and me in various ways. To cite just one example, he was very vigilant to make sure we didn't so much as step on his property, yet he would repeatedly steal the gravel from our new driveway and put it on his. As a Christian I knew I should love my neighbor. But try as I might, I found that I could not conjure up any love in my heart for this man.

Now, we can do things that look like love, and act lovingly, but that isn't necessarily the real thing. Genuine love springs spontaneously from the heart, and we know that it cannot be produced on command. So why would God command us to love, knowing that it cannot be commanded into existence or produced by force or fear? Why did He issue a law that appears to be imposed? And when He did it, why the awesome display of might and power?

One of the most important truths of Scripture is that God always speaks to us human beings in a language and manner we can understand. What happened between God and the Israelites at Sinai is a prime example. After centuries of exposure to idol worship in Egypt, the Israelites had almost completely lost sight of the true and living

God and His character of love. All the gods with whom they were acquainted were to be feared, not loved. And as slaves they were accustomed to imposed rules and forced obedience. They knew from experience that whoever was the most powerful, ruled, and they'd better obey—or else.

So when they got to Sinai, God met them on their level of understanding. In a terrible display of might and power, He shook the ground under their feet, and amid fire, smoke, lightning, and threat of death, thundered out ten commands. This demonstration of raw power was like nothing they'd ever seen before, and it scared the daylights out of them. They were so terrified they begged Moses: "You speak to us, and we will listen; but do not let God speak to us or we will die" (Exod. 20:19, NRSV). In issuing the law amid threats and in the form of imposed rules, God was simply speaking a language they could understand. And you can believe He got their attention!

Then God proposed an agreement. Their part was to obey, and without hesitation they said, "All that the Lord has spoken we will do, and we will be obedient" (Exod. 24:7, NRSV). Now given their background and what they had just witnessed, their response is understandable. But did they keep their part? Are you kidding? Only a few weeks later, they cast off their allegiance to God and worshiped a statue of a calf!

If God knows the future—and I believe He does—why would He propose an agreement that He knew wouldn't be kept? Why would He give them the Ten Commandments, ordering them to love, knowing they were incapable of doing it on their own? The first clue is found in their response: "All that the Lord has spoken *we* will do, *we* will obey." They readily agreed because they thought they could keep their part of the bargain. They didn't know they couldn't. So God, the consummate teacher, gave them the opportunity to try, so that in failing they would come to realize their utter inability to obey and their need of Him.

Secondly, after the rebellion in Eden, people, of themselves, could no longer love in a mature way. In fact, their natural tendencies were just the opposite. If people were ever to experience any degree of peace, harmony, and happiness, they must have practical instructions on how to relate to God and their fellow humans. And though they could not love in a mature way, if they at least externally followed the instructions, they could escape some of the negative consequences of their unloving ways. It would help them to live in harmony with their neighbor and their God until God could write the law in their hearts and bring them back into full harmony with the principles of love.

When Christ came in person, He again commanded love. Although He called it a "new commandment," it's the same law embodied in the Ten Commandments. So the law has not changed. And it's clear that our situation hasn't changed either. In the same sentence in which He commanded love, Christ gave us the solution: "I am the vine, and you are the branches. Those who remain in me, and I in them, will bear much fruit; for you can do nothing without me" (John 15:5, GNB). Turning to the book of Hebrews, the Lord is paraphrased as saying, "I will write my laws in their minds so they will know what I want them to do without my even telling them, and these laws will be in their hearts so they will want to obey them, and I will be their God and they shall be my people" (Heb. 8:10, LB). And Paul makes it even clearer, "For it is God who is producing in you both the desire and the ability to do what pleases him" (Phil. 2:13, ISV).

Friends, "come near to God, and he will come near to you. Wash your hands, you sinners. Make your hearts pure, you who can't make up your minds" (James 4:8, NIrV). "So let's do it—full of belief, confident that we're presentable inside and out" (Heb. 10:22, MSG).

Bibliography

Harvey, Van A. *A Handbook of Theological Terms.* New York: Touchstone, Simon and Schuster, 1964.

Phillips, Michael R. *Knowing The Heart of God.* Minneapolis, MN: Bethany House Publishers, 1990.

Webster's New Collegiate Dictionary. Springfield, MA: G. and C. Merriam Company, 1997.

We invite you to view the complete
selection of titles we publish at:

www.TEACHServices.com

Scan with your mobile
device to go directly
to our website.

Please write or email us your praises, reactions, or
thoughts about this or any other book we publish at:

P.O. Box 954
Ringgold, GA 30736
info@TEACHServices.com

TEACH Services, Inc., titles may be purchased in bulk
for educational, business, fund-raising,
or sales promotional use.
For information, please e-mail:

BulkSales@TEACHServices.com

Finally, if you are interested in seeing
your own book in print, please contact us at

publishing@TEACHServices.com

We would be happy to review your manuscript for free.

www.ingramcontent.com/pod-product-compliance
Lightning Source LLC
Chambersburg PA
CBHW070544170426
43200CB00011B/2554